SO YOU WANT TO BE A POP STAR

How to make *your* dreams of fame come true

Martin Roach

*Dedicated to my beautiful wife, Kaye,
with whom it is a delight to share my life.*

First published in Great Britain in 2003 by
Virgin Books Ltd
Thames Wharf Studios
Rainville Road
London
W6 9HA

ISBN 0 7535 0769 2

Typeset by Phoenix Photosetting, Chatham, Kent
Printed and bound in Great Britain by Mackays of Chatham

CONTENTS

FOREWORD

You have to really want to do this.

You have to be born to do it.

It will take over your life.

It's a vocation, like being a priest or a nun. Once you are in the music business, you've got the bug and there's no turning back. It can be a hard business at times – you will have to toughen yourself up and be able to take rejection. There's an awful lot of rejection in the music business and it can be the hardest thing to take. Just look at the casualties. I've had rejection all my life – I'm still getting it – but, if you believe in yourself and in whatever you do, then just go for it. It's all part of growing up, getting to know how the music business works and listening to the right people.

It's going to be really hard work, too. You can't buy this: you just have to go through it. All the top stars work incredibly hard. Bono works hard, Bon Jovi works hard. No matter who they are, stars graft constantly. If you're lazy, you're in the wrong business. This is the biggest misconception I see about the pop world. It's glamorous for about five minutes when you sing on *Top of the Pops*, but what it will have taken to get you there is certainly not glamorous.

Look at Elton John. He looked wrong, he wasn't a sex symbol, he wasn't even a lead singer. He was the piano player for Long John Baldry. But he worked hard, he wrote songs, he played live, kept reinventing himself and has rightly been a superstar for thirty years.

You will need luck, too. It's like having a lottery ticket – it's that much of a long shot. But, if you can just keep at it, you will increase your chances.

Get the right people around you, be they your fellow band members or those working for you. Top pop acts live on top of each other, do support tours together, slog together, sing, grovel, cry and dance together. That chemistry with your band or your management will get you through the times when there's no hope. Remember, everyone gets those difficult times, without exception: Elton John, David Bowie, George Michael, Ronan Keating and Westlife . . .

You will need to be aware of the problems. You *will* become public property. Read a little about the music business, find out how it works, and be determined to educate yourself in how to succeed and what can happen if you do.

Above all, keep your feet firmly on the ground, never give up and, more than anything else, believe in yourself. You have to have belief, belief, belief.

– *Louis Walsh, September 2002*

ABOUT THE AUTHOR

Described by *Melody Maker* as 'the biographer of youth culture and music' and by *Record Collector* as 'a publishing prodigy', Martin Roach has written 82 books in ten years, amassing more than 2 million global sales. His professional background is a degree in historical research from Warwick University. Since then, Roach has established his own music-publishing house, Independent Music Press, as a specialist in first-to-the-market biographies of major bands. More recently he started IMP Fiction with his publisher wife, Kaye. In addition, he has ghostwritten numerous celebrities' autobiographies. Please feel free to send him your queries by checking out his website: www.impbooks.com.

ACKNOWLEDGMENTS

In the course of writing this book I have been constantly amazed and delighted at how helpful, positive and knowledgeable all of the contributors have been. I thank and salute all of them sincerely. In alphabetical order, my warmest gratitude is extended to: Danielle Bardega at SBM, Stephen Barnes at Upshot, Andrew Borge, Cate Brown at EMI, Stephen Budd at SBM, Brian Cannon at Microdot, Julian Carreras at Hall Or Nothing, Mike Champion, Karen Christie at Mushroom, Dave Clark at DPC, Philip Conway, Bruce Craigie, Stuart David and Looper, Dawsons Music in Warrington, Bethan Elfyn, John Fairs, Iain Forsyth, Dan Frampton, Paul Franklin, Andy Franks, Jill Furmanovsky, Jessica Garlick, Malcolm Garrett, Hugh Goldsmith and Innocent Records, Carrie and David Grant, Sue Hall, Damian Harris at Skint, Nigel Hassler at Helter Skelter, Terry Hollingsworth and Global Entertainment Ltd, Liam Howlett and the Prodigy, Paul Hutton at Metropolis, Florence Irwin, Dave James at the Band Agency, Martin James, Mike James and Alan Arnison Entertainment Consultancy, Tracy Jay, Stephen Jones, Louise Kattenhorn, Martin Lamb, Jonathan Lattimer, Korda Marshall at Mushroom, Nik Moore at Work Hard, Mat Morrisroe, Paul Oakenfold, Olly and Little Joe Zero, Oskar Paul, Gary Pettet at MFL, Craig Pilling, Cordelia Plunket, Jane Pollard, Ange Potter, David Rowell at Echo, Stuart Slater at Virgin Books, Albert Samuel and Richard Smith at Mission Control, Duane Thornborough and Elite Entertainment (MCR) Ltd, Tony Wadsworth at EMI, Ben Wardle, Westlife, Dylan White at Anglo, Nick White at Smash Press, Darrin Woodford at Echo, Sylvia Young.

Legal text provided by Rupert Sprawson, Michelle Brown and Nigel Gilroy of Davenport Lyons.

Many thanks to Richard Carman for the 'oil painting'.

Special thanks to Louis Walsh for the Foreword.

INTRODUCTION

ACKNOWLEDGMENTS

Two of my best moments in music were watching the Sex Pistols at Finsbury Park in 1996 and then, six years later, jumping off my sofa when Will Young pipped Gareth Gates to the crown of *Pop Idol* (my 24 phone votes must have made a difference). An odd mix, perhaps, and maybe not one that might be considered cool. But there you have it. I am a punk freak and a pop lover.

I think anyone who wants to be a pop star is slightly unbalanced. It's a mad, weird and wonderful world and I admire you enormously. I know what you're up against. Watching these TV audition shows, standing at the back of hundreds of sweaty gigs, hearing comments in record company receptions. This happens to me all the time and through this book I hope to explain how these errors can be either controlled or avoided altogether. I will explain in depth all the major elements of what you need to know or achieve to become a pop star. I will also intentionally shatter the multitude of illusions that people have about a life in pop. This is a job, a profession, not a holiday camp.

There are two clear paths that you will encounter along your journey. Either you aspire to be a pop star – the next Will Young or Steps, maybe – or you are more inspired by the rock world, playing your own instruments and reading magazines like *NME*. I have tried to straddle the two genres, but in many ways they constantly dovetail anyway. There are so many tips and ideas that could work for both career paths, so, whether or not you find manufactured pop not to your liking, you should read every sentence in this book.

Of course, the quickest route to fame is to audition for *Pop Idol* or any other TV audition show. Better still, make this your first ever audition and then, when you win, you will have avoided a whole heap of work. Of course, in reality, becoming a pop star is infinitely much harder than this. It will be the hardest goal you ever try to achieve. You need to know *so* much.

You might ask why I am writing a book with the title *So You Want To Be A Pop Star* when I am not a pop star myself. There are two very good reasons. First, I am a *failed* pop star, as so many people in the music industry are. However, I am not a failed pop star who thinks that those who made it are lucky. I know that virtually everyone you see on *Top of the Pops* deserves it.

I didn't make it because I wasn't good enough. I was in a punk band called the Chocolate Speedway Riders. We wrote songs such as 'Every Time I See You, My Pacemaker Skips a Beat' and lived above a dingy shop in north London, working in a textile factory by day and assaulting the ears of as many unfortunate gig-goers as possible by night.

We never made it, but that ramshackle outfit provided me with some of the best days of my life, as well as many of the hardest-working. I will enlighten you more on the Chocolate Speedway Riders as we work through this book together, particularly when I need to highlight specific mistakes. We made a lot of those! Looking back, we were probably never going to make it, but the lessons I learned from being in a band full-time for three years were priceless, and I want to share them with you.

Second, I may not be a pop star, but I do have access to a lot of people who are, or work with, pop stars. Despite what you might hear or think, the music business is inhabited by many people brimming with immense expertise, who freely gave me their generous assistance and offered lashings of encouragement for pop hopefuls. By compiling this book, I am trying to pass their wisdom over to you.

This is no guaranteed guide to becoming a pop star, there is no such thing. 'X-factor' is something you either have or you don't. I recognise that unconditionally. By writing this book I am not attempting to suggest there is a formula for being a pop star, despite what the harshest critics say about some aspects of the music business. Instead, *So You Want To Be A Pop Star* is an attempt to collect together years and years of wisdom from the people who know best: the stars, their managers, record companies, agents, bookers, press officers, lawyers, accountants and all the other small but essential cogs that go into making the music business the incendiary, vibrant and enthralling world that it is.

Enough said. Time to get on with the show.

1. THE BOTTOM LINE

'I won't be happy until I am as famous as God.' Madonna

'To get anywhere in this business, you have to be tough and clever. Talent is only half the battle.' Dolores O'Riordan of the Cranberries

So you want to be a pop star. At some point in our lives, many of us do. However, before you plunge into the murky depths of pop, you need to ask yourself a few searching questions. Do you want to be a pop star or, more likely, do you just want to be famous? Do you crave the opportunity to confront your insecurities in front of several thousand people, or are you more concerned that they applaud and adore you regardless? Do you want the satisfaction of releasing a classic record that becomes a pivotal moment in music history or do you want bags of cash, fast cars and boys/girls?

Personally, as far as that last question is concerned, I went for the latter. Why not? A little adoration never hurt anybody; a fleet of limos and supercars is always handy; and the pages of countless entertainment magazines confirmed my suspicions that all pop stars lead fantastic lives filled with endless parties, designer clothes and the occasional celebrity-studded show at the Royal Albert Hall. That was my first and probably most crucial mistake.

So, before we look at what you will have to go through if you are to stand even the slightest chance of becoming a pop star, you need to be aware of a few harsh realities. You will read about these in more depth throughout every chapter of this book, but they are so essential to your success that I want to highlight them here first. Ignore these home truths and either your heart or your dreams – and most probably both – will be shattered.

1. THE TALENT

This is at the very heart of your chance to become a pop star. An obvious and simple point yet one that is so often ignored. Do you have talent? *Real* talent? That buzzword, 'X-factor'? The sort of talent that inspires mass hysteria in thousands of young people while thousands more glaze over in adoration? Very, very few people actually do. The reason that ten thousand hopefuls queue for an audition and only two make it into the charts is simply because the vast majority of that snaking line of wannabes just do not have the talent.

Be objective about yourself, be critical and be realistic. If you still think you have the voice/looks/songs/ability, then read on.

2. HOW BADLY DO YOU WANT IT?
Badly? *How* badly? Unless you're already involved in the pop world, you can't possibly comprehend the long hours, personal pressures, private intrusions and combined mental and physical demands involved. You probably watch S Club 7 on *Top of the Pops* and think, 'Look how fresh and bubbly they are – they can't be working *that* hard. . .' What you don't know is they are probably at the wrong end of an eighteen-hour day and it's three weeks since their last half-day off. In trying to become a pop star, you will have to make many sacrifices and if you succeed – and I sincerely hope you do – then those sacrifices will have only just begun. So it's vitally important that from a very early stage you are under no illusion about exactly what you're letting yourself in for.

3. BELIEVE IN YOURSELF
How can you shake off the countless rejections and disappointments that will inevitably come your way, even if you are the next Michael Jackson? *You have to believe in yourself.* If you don't think you're the greatest, how can you expect anyone else to? However, don't mistake self-confidence for arrogance. One is an inspiration, the other a millstone.

4. THE MUSIC BUSINESS IS A *BUSINESS*
You're attempting to work in one of the most cutthroat, cruel and competitive industries that exist. If you are to succeed in the business of music, you will need to be a good salesperson. Every time you sing, talk, dance or just walk into a room, you are selling yourself. Michael Stipe, lead singer with REM, once said, 'Of course I'm a commodity. I know that. And I'm fine with it. Really.' You're taking your talent and your art and offering it up for meticulous inspection in front of people whose job it is to make money. There will be times when this clash between art and business will seem just unbearable. If you already insist that under no circumstances will you shave off that goatee beard because it is the lifeblood of your talent – and, like Samson's strength,

which he said was in his hair, will seep away to nothing without it – then perhaps you'd better stop right now and put this book down (especially if you're a woman!). If you're to become a pop star – and *stay* a pop star – many decisions will have to be made that are business decisions, not artistic statements. Not all of the time, but quite often. Think about that.

In addition, like any aspiring businessperson, you'd better be painstakingly professional. Preparation, practice, presentation, persistence: dismiss any of these crucial professional qualities and you can forget it. The pop world can be an uncertain and highly subjective place to inhabit, but one fact is set in stone – if you're not professional, you won't be there for long, if ever. Keep your eyes on the prize.

5. DON'T GIVE UP!
Ever!

2. GETTING STARTED

'Keep your nose clean and your chin up, even if it requires surgery.'
Ray Davies, the Kinks

GAINING VOCAL CONFIDENCE

Singing in the shower or in front of the bedroom mirror with a hairbrush is usually where it all starts for most aspiring pop stars. You've got your favourite CDs that you sing along to, thinking you're a natural, but how does it actually sound? There's one way of finding out: sing in public.

An obvious place to get your very first public singing experience is at school. There may be music classes where you can volunteer to showcase yourself. In all likelihood, the school will put on musical productions throughout the year. Put yourself forward for all of these shows. Or perhaps you and some of your like-minded friends sing together, either at school or back in your bedrooms.

Where do the majority of people sing in public every week? In church choirs. This needn't be all boring sermons, flowing robes and candlelit masses. Importantly, you will regularly sing a variety of music, quite often of a demanding range. You will learn about adhering to melody, disciplining yourself to complement other voices, exercising vocal control and educating yourself in harmony and structure. You will start to gain confidence in front of an audience and meet other people with a passion for music.

Before you complain about aching buttocks on wooden pews and trying to keep your eyes open at the back, remember this: choir singers *do* go on to become global superstars. Many pop, soul and R&B acts learned their trade and literally found their voice through the church – Justin Timberlake and Whitney Houston being just two examples. Don't think that this avenue will confine you to singing only in front of spinsters and the Women's Institute. Good choirs get invited to perform at a wide variety of social functions in front of sizeable audiences. Renowned choirs even get involved in tours both at home and abroad. It might not be Party in the Park or Ozzfest, but it is invaluable experience. There is also a thriving and competitive circuit of choir events that provide many pop stars with their first taste of life on the road. All of these benefits aside, I am not suggesting that you cynically join your local church choir to earn experience for your gangsta rap outfit. Heaven forbid! (And they probably will.) One final word of advice worth bearing in mind about church choirs – you might find your pastor won't be too overjoyed if you throw his telly out of the belfry.

KARAOKE

'Karaoke is a good way of practising but it won't develop your own sense of identity. The real talent from Pop Idol was not out singing on a karaoke machine every week.' – Carrie Grant, vocal coach to stars such as Will Young, the Spice Girls and Gareth Gates

Karaoke is a worldwide entertainment phenomenon, but is it any use to you as a budding pop star? The word 'karaoke' is derived from the Japanese for 'empty orchestra' and is probably the only word of that language known to the millions who perform at karaoke nights in pubs, clubs, hotels and cafés all over the world. In the first instance, you can buy very affordable karaoke machines with backing CDs to practise at home until you're old enough to go to bars. Why not invite your friends round and make a night of it?

Outside the safety net of your bedroom, on any night of the year, in any town in the world, it seems that you can stand up and be a three-minute superstar. Karaoke provides an easily accessible opportunity to practise your voice, gain confidence in front of an audience and develop your stage presence and style. Some venues take karaoke a step further with organised competitions.

For many people, karaoke is the first chance they get to sing in public, *but* this is probably also where it stops being useful, for two reasons. First, karaoke can give you a false sense of your own ability. The crowd will invariably contain friends of yours in differing states of inebriation as well as strangers who are there to have a good night out. Belting out Elvis Presley's 'American Trilogy' at 2 a.m. to wild applause does not mean you will be competing with Kylie for the Christmas number one. Second, karaoke tends to encourage impersonation. You want to be a pop star, not a tribute act.

The key to karaoke is to see it for what it is. Occasionally, it might lead you on to bigger and better things, but most of the time you'll simply have fun, practise your singing and be cheered off stage by your mates.

SINGING LESSONS

With a little practice under your belt, you might start to think about sending off a cassette or CD to industry insiders. Don't. Remember this: you get only one opportunity to impress and, chances are, you're not ready yet. You will have to work incredibly hard to create maybe just one slender opportunity, so you need to maximise your potential and get yourself some singing lessons.

Have you ever read a passage from a book out loud? Have you noticed how quickly you get out of breath? Well, singing live or in a studio is a thousand times worse than that. Singing lessons will give you a basic grounding of technique, otherwise you might find yourself fainting in front of Pete Waterman.

All the top pop stars have used vocal teachers and coaches. You only need to watch *Pop Idol* to see the benefits of just a few hours with Carrie and David Grant, pop's premier vocal coaches, to understand the importance of this premise. Have you ever thought, 'I wish I could sit down with Carrie Grant for an afternoon and ask her loads of questions'? Well, I did and this is how our conversation went . . .

MR: Assuming that readers of this book can't afford to call you up or hire you, is it worth their getting local singing lessons?

CG: Lessons normally cost about £12 an hour and it might be good to take one or two a month rather than weekly. Often, a teacher who's been in the music industry is a better idea than someone who's only ever been a teacher. So, yes, singing lessons are good, but keep an open mind as well. Having time away from those lessons, to really think about what's been discussed and explained, is a really good idea. Tape your exercises and work on them at home. That can help keep costs down too.

MR: OK, but whenever I taped myself at home I sounded like Frank Skinner impersonating Cliff Richard.

CG: You must always remember that taping your own voice never sounds as good on playback. How you sound in your own head is never the same in the real world, either.

MR: This is true. I've been told by many people I actually sound like Frank Skinner impersonating Darren Day. What if singing lessons are not an option, either through availability or cost? Does this mean I will never be a pop star?

CG: No. One of the ways that you can learn is by singing along to bands you love. That can help develop and nurture vocal identity. But be careful. What you don't want at all costs is pastiche, because then it just becomes karaoke. You need to develop your own style, so listen to a broader spectrum of singers. Don't just focus on Britney and sound exactly like her. By the time you've get enough experience to present yourself to a record company, they'll already have fifteen Britneys trying to get signed. Plus, by then Britney herself has already moved on, so it just looks dated. One of the most beautiful things about creativity is that it's totally unique to each person, but if you don't see it as that you can slowly become the person you admire.

MR: Can you recommend exercises to do at home?

CG: The best thing that you can do to warm up your voice is humming. Vocal cords are basically two little flaps of skin, a muscle if you like, so they need warming up. If you got out of bed and suddenly flung your leg over your head, you'd hurt yourself! So if you hurl your voice straight into some mad, screaming note like a top 'C', you will similarly do yourself damage. So hum some low notes, some notes in the middle and some higher stuff to warm up.

MR: If I start practising at home then, should I buy a microphone to use? My hairbrush is getting worn out.

CG: I would advise never to sing into a mike when you're practising technique. You really need to hear how the voice is sounding and a mike can make you think you're sounding great when in fact you're not. Microphone technique is something separate you need to learn later. You see so many people pick up a microphone and instantly go into a karaoke vibe, pulling the mike away for the high and loud notes. You don't need to do that – with today's equipment you should keep your mouth by the mike at all times. You need to work all that out.

MR: Music legend has it that the R&B vocalist Shola Ama was discovered singing walking through a tube station. Her friends said she sang more than she talked. How much should I be practising?

CG: If a singer needs to be asked to practise, then they won't make it. The more you sing, the stronger your voice will get – it's a muscle, so use it. If people are saying, 'Will you please shut up!' then you're obviously inspired to sing all the time!

MR: Assuming I've had a few lessons, what advice can you give me about singing live?

CG: You need to be aware of the different environments you can sing in. In a studio, for example, the quality of the mikes means you can sing very quietly and add an intimacy that you can't invoke live when you're running up and down the stage. It's not necessarily different technique, more about the style of singing. Having said that, many modern artists do run and jump all over the stage all night while singing live! Singing at a local venue, you'll have vocals piped through monitors on the front of the stage. This is when so many singers lose their voices because they can't control things as easily. If you get signed, you will start using an earpiece for your own vocal monitor so things will get easier.

MR: Do you have any specific tips about looking after your voice?

CG: Diet is important and often overlooked. Dairy products are not good for your voice, so a lot of people cut out chocolate and cheese. They cause phlegm, which makes you cough, which in turn is hopeless for your singing. This has the dual purpose of keeping you slim!

MR: I was out late last night and have picked up a stinking cold. My head's pounding. But will that make me sound like Burt Bacharach in today's audition?

CG: Proper technique – without losing your identity – can help you avoid these problems, even if you get struck down with a cold. There are some tips to remedy such symptoms too. For example, ginger is a good anti-inflammatory. If your throat gets sore, put ginger in your tea, the particles will infuse in there and work wonders. Also, putting your head over a steaming bowl of boiling water is a great help. Do that twice a day to really take down the swelling.

MR: I smoke forty fags a day and I still can't get that gravely growl of Joe Cocker. Should I up it to sixty a day or try more heavy tar?

CG: Smoking is really, *really* bad for your throat. There's no other way of saying it. You need to appreciate the biology of what happens when you talk or sing. Vocal cords control the air that is going into your lungs. They flap and beat together about a hundred and eighty times a second. Can you imagine the nicotine and all that rubbish going over those chords a hundred and eighty times a second, in and out? Smoking also dries out your vocal cords. That can't be good for your throat, your lungs or your cords. To the rock-and-rollers who say, 'Yes, but listen to the gravel,' I would say, 'Yes, and listen to the price of the surgery in a few years.' You may well be on the way to severe nodules, which are like blisters on your vocal cords. If you have shoes that don't fit properly they will rub you and cause blisters. In the same way, your vocal cords can get damaged. Nodules can totally finish your career, period.

MR: What's the difference between singing lessons and vocal coaching?

CG: Singing teaching is slightly different. I personally feel that you need someone to understand your future pop career, not just ask you to sing scales. Having said that, singing teachers can be very helpful, especially if you find that magical person who is in tune with your aspirations. A vocal coach, on the other hand, does two things. Firstly, they give you a technique that should last throughout your whole career, enabling you to do everything from recording in the studio, live work, harmonies, TV, every aspect of an artist's life. That variety of singing work all requires a technique that means you will not lose your voice. Secondly, for David and me working within the pop industry, we look to really bring the artist's *identity* out. We don't want them to end up sounding like an opera singer or a West End performer, so we work slightly differently from a normal vocal teacher. For example, if you were teaching U2's Bono before he was signed, you would say, 'I want to keep all of his identity, but we need to teach him certain things so he can safely sing six nights a week and not lose his voice.'

MR: What are the most common mistakes a singer can make – apart from being rubbish?

CG: Trying too hard. Oversinging, overkilling, they need to lay back more and learn how to *sell* a song. Great music is soul music. By soul, I don't mean just black R&B music, but when people sing from the heart, like Bono or the Counting Crows. They make you say, 'That is an amazing vocal, it moves me.' Those vocalists use a lot of underselling, so that, when they come to the part that is killing them to sing, that touches you even more. If someone stands there and thinks, 'I have to impress you with my vocals,' it will never be as good as someone thinking, 'I've got sell this song to you. I'm selling a story.' A song is just a story that has a melody to it and to tell that with passion needs more sensitivity. That doesn't necessarily mean you have to be technically meticulous. Bono always sounds like his vocal cords are literally bleeding, but I love his voice, so much soul. Besides, he must have technique because he sings many nights a week. What about David Bowie? Another great singer with his own style and unique identity. Try to learn from that, although to some degree you've either got it or you haven't.

MR: How can a vocal coach contribute to a pop hopeful getting noticed?

CG: The essence of making it in the pop business is about being unique, a one-off. My goal is to make the artist absolutely individual and bring out their flavour, their X-factor. David and I have got forty years in the industry between us and we see that X-factor at a glance. Take Will Young: he has so much identity. You only need to hear him sing two words and you know it's Will's voice, which is something amazing for someone who was so recently an unknown. We spotted it early on in *Pop Idol*. Will had only just scraped through to the final fifty – he'd been stuck in the 'maybe room' all day. Yet, immediately on hearing him, we thought 'Oh my gosh, this guy is amazing!' So we told the producers, 'We think we've found your Pop Idol.'

MR: Is part of your role about harnessing more than just untapped vocal potential?

CG: Our teaching is focused on much more than just singing: we look at performance and all manner of different elements. I believe a record company will look for three key factors: your choice of songs, your image and your voice. Are those three components all sending out the same message? Remember, record company executives are marketing people, so, if those three elements contradict in any way, they will not understand. Therefore, there's no point us taking someone who is really grungy and turning them into R&B.

MR: Can you find things out about your talent through working with a vocal coach that you maybe didn't realise existed? For example, in my case, that I haven't got any talent.

CG: Yes. Let's use Gareth Gates as an example. People think of him as this airy, gentle performer, but they don't realise he can sing incredibly strongly. When we coached Gareth through 'Proms in the Park', we were doing vocal exercises and I uncovered this phenomenal voice. People don't realise he actually trained as a classical singer and has got this massive voice. Yet he has grown up modelling himself on acts such as Westlife and Boyzone. When I heard this classical vocal, I said, 'Right, Gareth, I've heard that now. We're going to get some of that tone into your new pop material.' He was only using about thirty per cent of his ability. He knew this but didn't know how to put it across to his pop audience.

MR: You've worked with the Spice Girls. Are there any lessons to be learned from them?

CG: When people come out of bands and go solo it can be very difficult: they're used to working with other members. Melanie C did all this shouting and ad-lib stuff in the Spice Girls but the first sessions with her were a revelation – what a great voice, a really lovely tone. I've seen her twice a week for two years. She constantly works exceptionally hard. That's an important lesson if you want to be a great singer. Here was a member of the biggest girl band of all time who was so driven and perfectionist that she was still looking to improve herself. Vocal coaching and singing lessons are an ongoing process, don't rest on your laurels . . . ever.

So there is your one-on-one with Carrie Grant. Don't say you haven't been warned . . .

STAGE SCHOOL

Another possible route to the big time that you may want to consider is attending stage school. You would typically be anywhere between nine and sixteen years old, but obviously this differs from school to school. There are many schools available all over the country, so do your research well. The costs can vary, too, and it can be expensive – so be careful. There are also some excellent nationally networked schools, such as Stagecoach, which can bring the chance to attend stage school mainly part-time directly into your area. There are branches of Stagecoach all over the country and this can be a superb way of seeing if a more formal approach to your career is suitable for you.

To give you an idea of what a stage school can offer you, I spoke to the most famous name in the business, Sylvia Young. Her school actually focuses more heavily on acting, and is not a 'pop school' as such. Nevertheless, the skills you will learn are as universally useful for aspiring pop stars as for acting hopefuls.

A huge number of the faces we see acting on our TV screens every night hail from Sylvia's stable. Sam Janus (*Game On*) started out with Sylvia, as did Nick Berry, star of *Heartbeat*. Much of the cast of *Hollyoaks* and *Family Affairs* and many of the cast of *EastEnders* did, too, including Sharon Watts, Robbie Jackson, Gus and Billy Mitchell. More to the point of this book, however, are the successes of former Sylvia Young School pupils who have become famous in the music business: Emma Bunton of the Spice Girls, Billie Piper, Jon Lee from S Club, the Appleton sisters and Melanie Blatt.

WHY GO TO STAGE SCHOOL?
Your local comprehensive school is understandably unlikely to teach you the discipline of taking direction, how to behave in a studio or in front of an audition panel. Therefore, if you want more coaching than this at a young age, then maybe stage school is one option for you.

Three days of every week, Sylvia's pupils are taught purely academic subjects while the remaining two days are split among drama, song and dance, with the emphasis on acting. Stage school thrusts you into an environment where the focus of everyone around you is to succeed in the performing arts. 'Being with other talented people undoubtedly spurs you on,' explains Sylvia. 'There is a certain amount of competitiveness between pupils, but because they are friends this is not as harsh as they will experience in the outside world.'

Sylvia is also at pains to instil realism into her students. 'It may be wonderful to get a deal or a contract, but we equip our pupils to take it more in their stride. It is what they expect, rather than being tremendously overawed and excited.' Similarly, the school reinforces the positivity that needs to be a constant feature of any aspiring pop star's career. She continues:

We try to make the students understand that if they are rejected for a job it is not their talent that is being questioned, but more a case of just not being what the director is looking for at that specific time or for that specific role. We nurture in our students that rejection is just not being right for that particular job.

Another benefit of stage school is that you're likely to have better access to some of the tools of the music trade. Sylvia's school has a small recording studio, something most normal schools are unable to provide. If any of her pupils want to put something down on CD, this facility is made available to them.

Our head of music works with these kids and gives up freely of his time, so that they can get the experience of being in the studio. Very often it will be a pop song that they use or something they've written themselves. Our priority, however, is to train the ear and enable them to hold harmonies. They learn this very fast at our school – it is something we expect.

An obvious core benefit of stage school is the breadth of the disciplines you will learn. Sylvia's students take various style of dance class, which provides an invaluable grounding, especially as the role of dance is becoming increasingly vital in a modern pop performer. 'You can have the greatest voice in the world,' she says, 'but if you don't have dance ability there are very few musicals where you have a chance. Some auditions for singing parts in the musicals may even ask you to dance first.' OK, while you may not be aiming for a part in a West End show, you can benefit hugely by being trained to such high standards.

This doesn't mean to say that without stage-school guidance you can't learn and then refine your dancing skills. Sylvia insists that there are some great local dance schools that can equip you just as well for a career involving dance. 'Here we can only do a limited amount,' she explains, 'because we have only two days to split between everything – speech, drama, improvisation, ballet, jazz, tap – so if you go to a local dance school you might actually get as much or far more training.'

One reason why Sylvia's students often end up as pop stars is because they have trained their voices to a standard that is appropriate to a career in West End stage shows. In almost all instances, this means they are more than adequately equipped for a pop career. Interestingly, specific audition coaching is not what you might think. 'Although the process always varies, we try basically not to coach for auditions unless it is something specific, where they must know a particular song for a musical or they must have a particular dialect. In general, we like our pupils to be as natural as possible.'

HOW DO I ENROL?

If by now you're convinced this is the avenue for you, you need to be aware that competition for places is fierce. At Sylvia Young's, the average yearly intake totals about 25. Around eight hundred will audition for those elusive places at the school of their dreams. What are they looking for that will persuade them to make you one of the chosen few?

Surprisingly, perhaps, the very first task you're asked to complete by Sylvia is an academic test. She goes on to explain why.

We aren't looking for brilliant academics but we are looking for kids who are of average academic intelligence or above. It's a hard timetable here – remember that three days are academic and only two days are vocational. The three days of academic are tough and, if days are missed because of a professional work commitment, that child has to be academically bright enough and focused enough to catch up.

You will then be asked to present your vocational skills to the dance and song departments before – last but by no means least – you're given an acting piece to learn. So do they expect you to be tremendously gifted in all of these areas? 'When we really analyse prospective students, we are generally looking for acting ability. The kids have to show some potential for the acting world, because we believe that acting is the core foundation that an all-round career is built on.'

Sylvia is also keen to emphasise that successful artists, whether actors, West End performers or pop stars, should always be looking to continue to learn. 'We encourage pupils to think about all the areas as a profession, not just performance. The difficulty is that they leave us at sixteen and will often have go on to further training before they are successful. Although we have had people go straight into the West End or a pop career from here, it is more likely that you will need further training to develop the voice, and further dance lessons.'

Sylvia Young is a remarkable lady. She is widely acknowledged as being at the peak of her profession and a genuine maker of stars, yet, with so many success stories to boast of, she insists on making one final point.

A lot of these former pupils have done it for themselves, you know. People assume that the Sylvia Young School has made all these things happen. Maybe we have instilled into them a core of important values and skills, but in the majority of cases they have ultimately gone out and made it happen themselves. Whether you got stage school or not, it is all about determination, talent and focus.

Wise words indeed – forget them at your peril.

3. BEFORE YOU GO INTO A STUDIO

'We were so awkward, musically speaking, when we got together as a band. We couldn't really play our instruments or anything. But that didn't stop us from playing them.' Bono

'Yes, I do know what my songs are about. Some are about four minutes, some are about five and, believe it or not, some are about eleven or twelve.' Bob Dylan

TO PLAY OR NOT TO PLAY?

Very possibly, you're not interested in playing an instrument. With a voice like yours, you don't need one, right? However, are you aware that Gareth Gates is an accomplished guitarist? Did you know Darius wrote his debut number-one single 'Colourblind'? Are you aware A1 are all multi-instrumentalists? Even if you're adamant that you want only to sing, you should at least read this chapter and consider widening your musical abilities in light of the benefits that may result.

Do you need to play an instrument to be a pop star? It depends on what kind of a pop star you want to be. For example, Britney, Atomic Kitten and Jennifer Lopez don't play in their videos or on stage. Furthermore, if you're fortunate enough to sign a pure-pop-record deal, you will be working closely with studio producers, engineers, songwriters and session musicians, so it is unlikely you will need to spearhead the musical backtrack.

However, you're entering the business of pop, so it can do no harm to have a knowledge of musicality. As you will see elsewhere in this book, the more commitment you can show to managers, promoters, record companies and industry insiders, the more seriously they will take you. Even if you don't need to play an instrument to showcase your talent, if you *can*, then people will probably see you as a more complete musical prospect.

Oskar Paul is one of the world's top songwriters – his compositions include Will Young's debut single 'Anything Is Possible', which is the fastest-selling single in British chart history. He revealed to me that quite often the purest pop performers often have a surprising musical ability.

To read music definitely helps but it's not necessary if you just want to be a singer. To be able to play either guitar or piano is always helpful, too. Gareth Gates, for example, has a total passion for music and is a brilliant piano player. He is very musical and, when he's in the studio, he doesn't want to stop until he's completely happy with his performance. When you're giving him guidance, you can tell him which notes to sing and he knows instantly.

Carrie Grant agrees:

Gareth is quite scary actually. On tour, he will go up to all these amazing band members and say, 'Is that A-sharp minor?' He knows his music; he plays really well. Same with Will. When they recorded their duet, 'The Long and Winding Road', that was done all live. They used one camera shot and one live vocal – nothing dubbed at all. That's how good those two are.

That said, be flexible. A pop performer will not win over an audition panel because he can play a ropy version of a Kylie Minogue song on a six-string. When Darius Danesh tried to sing one of his own compositions at a *Pop Idol* audition but was barred from doing so, he politely accepted the panel's decision (ironically, he would have performed his debut self-penned number-one single). In the pop environment, you don't often need an instrument to prop you up. Indeed, on occasion it could well detract from your performance. Think ahead about the audition you're attending. What are they after? Will an instrument help or hinder your chances?

By contrast, if your ambition is to be part of a band, then playing an instrument is obviously a necessity. Guitar or piano/keyboard is probably your best choice of starter instrument: the rudiments of both are easier to learn, and they can be bought at a reasonable cost.

There are hundreds of 'learn to play' books on the market, available from your local music store or online. As with singing, it won't do any harm to pay for a few lessons if you can afford them, or you can check your local newspaper or ask in your nearest music store. However much you teach yourself, a few wise words from an expert can really help you jump fences.

Likewise, there are scores of books on the market with detailed advice on specific equipment and instrument requirements, but below is a summary of a few basic rules to follow. The basic indie/rock band has a drummer, guitarist, bass player and singer (who may also be one of the above). You could also include a second guitarist, a keyboard player, a DJ, a percussionist and so on, but these are the kinds of elements that you realise you need only once your basic band has figured out the direction and sound it wants.

WHAT EQUIPMENT DO WE NEED?

Here are the basics for simple guitar-based bands:

- electric guitars
- bass guitars
- drum kits
- microphones
- amplifiers
- PA systems

GUITARS

You can get by without electric guitars, but to play in front of an audience you need amplification and an electric guitar is the best way to get heard. Pay as little or as much as you can afford. A decent second-hand guitar from an advert in the newspaper might cost as little as £30, or you can spend £3,000 in a high street music store. As with any workman, the more you spend on your tools, the better job you'll make of your work – but not everyone can afford the best. If you don't know a lot about guitars, go into your music retailer and ask advice – they can show you inexpensive guitars and explain to you why a guitar for £500 might sound so much better.

You can hear what they sound like, feel the weight (important if you're going to be playing a lot) and listen as the experts demonstrate every conceivable sound that each guitar can make. Don't be intimidated by the fact that everyone seems to know much more than you do. Have you seen the guitar-shop sketch in the film *Wayne's World*? He's trying out a new six-string and is prevented from playing his favourite Led Zeppelin riff by a sign that says, 'No "Stairway To Heaven"'. This Zeppelin classic is the sort of staple self-indulgence that you might hear in a guitar shop populated by (long-haired) people whose sole purpose in life is to show off their fretboard skills. Just remember: if they were that good, they'd probably be on tour rather than in a basement shop making a teenage novice feel insecure.

Many stores accept second-hand guitars in part exchange for new ones, so, although they may only *seem* to sell expensive new ones, a cheaper second-hand option is often available. An older guitar often sounds better than a new one, but beware of those that are rotten, old or worn out. It doesn't really matter what the body of the guitar looks like: it's how it sounds and plays that matters.

The best-known makes – and they are safe bets if you can afford them – are brands such as Gibson and Fender. They also make cheaper guitars that are often excellent in themselves (Gibson, for instance, also produce Epiphone guitars, which are excellent copies of original Gibsons).

Some words of caution:

- Don't rush into buying a guitar, however excited you are by the prospect. Ask for advice, shop around, play on at least a dozen instruments before you make your choice.
- Don't buy through mail order without having played the guitar yourself: one guitar does not sound exactly like another, and every player has his or her own preferences.
- Spend as much as you can realistically afford to. Some people say what you can afford is the money you actually have in your pocket. Many retailers will offer a hire-purchase sale, so you can pay over two or three years for an instrument that you may otherwise not be able to afford in one go – but be *sensible*. If you work only on Saturdays, it's probably best not to put a deposit on the Les Paul Gold Top that Mark Knopfler played on tour with Dire Straits.

BASS GUITARS

The bass is very much a solid backbone of a band but, because it is generally perceived as less glamorous than the guitar, a good bass player is worth his or her weight in gold. Stuart David, formerly of the Brit Award-winners Belle & Sebastian and now front man for Looper, recommends bass guitar as a wise option.

I'd been playing in bands for some time and we couldn't find a new bassist, so I decided I'd learn that. I started playing on demos for songwriters and bands to get as much practice as I could, playing live shows, too.

One of the musicians whose stuff I was playing on was Stuart Murdoch. I was the only bass player he knew, so, even though the line-up of the rest of his band kept changing, I was always there.

When he was asked to make a record for the music course at Stow College in Glasgow, he put Belle & Sebastian together and produced the album, *Tigermilk*.

The electric bass differs from the electric guitar in that it has only four strings and these are tuned much lower than those of an ordinary guitar. The best-known bass manufacturer is Fender, who also make a range of less expensive models under the Squire label. Buying a bass follows pretty much exactly the same pattern as that for ordinary guitars. However, it is good advice to be aware that many old basses have suffered more knocks than most guitars, so be careful when buying second-hand. You are buying something that might make you a superstar millionaire, so take your time and make the right choice.

DRUMS
A good drummer will never be out of work. Most young bands fold and fail because they can't find a drummer, so sorting out this part of your band early is a great step forward. You can play 'real' drums, or alternatively – and this is as much a stylistic choice as a practical one – invest in an electronic kit such as those made by Yahama or Roland.

However, it is likely that anyone who gets really enthusiastic about drums will eventually want his or her own kit. A basic setup would include a bass drum (the large drum that stands on its side on the floor), a couple of tom-toms, a snare (the harsh-sounding drum that puts the strongest beat in a lot of great records) and a variety of cymbals, hi-hats and rides (various flat brass discs held on posts in the kit). As with guitars, you can spend a fortune on a drum kit, but second-hand it could cost anything from £50 to £200.

MICROPHONES
If you are a singer looking to invest in your own microphone, it will interest you to know there is an industry-standard model called the Shaw SMF8, which retails at between £90 and £150. If you are spending over £150, though, note that there are many other options open to you, and your local music retailer will advise on what is best for your needs. Also, before you buy, remember that many venues will supply their own microphones.

AMPLIFIERS

An amplifier, or amp, is the machine that takes the sound from your voice or instrument and amplifies it electronically so that the people at the back of the school hall – or at the back of Wembley Arena – can hear what you are doing. There are many different makes and styles: low-wattage practice amps, 100-watt stage gear, combos or separate amp/speaker setups, bass amplifiers and so on. For the beginner, this can be a nightmare, because you can't really judge a good amplifier until you can play your instrument through it. Getting good advice from your nearest retailer and local musicians is an unbeatable way to start.

Sometimes an old Vox combo will give you the best sound in the world with the right guitar, while a brand-new Laney 40-watt amp with a couple of effects pedals could also do the trick. Listen to the bands you like, and try – through gigs, photos, fan-club websites – to figure out what equipment they use to create their sound. Finding the right amplification for your instrument or voice is often as important as finding the right guitar or drum kit. Borrow from friends and happily waste entire Saturday afternoons in music shops asking to play through as many machines as you can – this is how you learn. Where possible, always play your own instrument through any amp you are trying out – that way you get consistent results and can make better judgments.

A note regarding amplification for drums: until you are playing sizeable venues, there is usually no need for amplification for a drum kit – it is loud enough on its own for most small venues.

PA SYSTEMS

You need to think very carefully before spending money on a PA because there is a high chance you will not use it as much as you suspected. At an early, unsigned level, whether you are a solo performer or a band, the venue will most likely have its own PA, even if it often leaves a lot to be desired.

A basic PA system for amplifying and projecting your voice can set you back between £700 and £800. As with anything, you can pay as much as you like. An HK Lucas 1000 PA system will cost around £1,500. Invest in good leads – there's no point in spending £1,000 only to buy the connecting cables cheaply in a DIY superstore (it sounds silly, but there are plenty of people who have done it!). This also applies to the leads for your guitars and other instruments.

Don't forget: if you spend a lot of money on a PA, who will transport it to each gig and how much will that cost? Yes, you cry, but I'll be able to use it throughout my career and therefore always control the beautiful instrument that is my voice. Er . . . no. By the time you're signed, the venues will have much bigger and better PA systems than yours, which will now be redundant.

SHOULD I WRITE ORIGINAL MATERIAL OR NOT?

There is a mythology that says that, unless you solely write all your own material, you are not a 'proper' star. Elvis didn't, Karen Carpenter didn't. Neither did Cliff Richard. Britney doesn't, Will and Gareth don't, Kylie doesn't . . .

You can write your own lyrics and have someone else write your music; but, if you want all the songwriting credit – and all the income from royalties – you need to write the words *and* the tunes.

Natalie Appleton, formerly a member of All Saints and now part of Appleton with her sister Nicole, says,

Write your own songs, be creative – this will help you control your career, rather than be controlled. If you don't write songs and create the music, you *will* be controlled. You have to believe in yourself and make your own choices. Don't let other people make those decisions for you. If you think that something is wrong then stick to your guns. Don't be manipulated.

Oskar Paul, one of the world's top songwriters, raises this crucial point.

It all depends on how good your songs are. If pop hopefuls write their own material, it can help if it's interesting, but if it's just rubbish and they insist then of course that can hinder their progress. In the beginning you just need to be open-minded, really. I would encourage everyone to have a go at a little bit of writing. Especially singers, who are often very adept with melody. As with anything else, good writing comes with practice. Very few are born great writers.

The question of original material predominantly but not exclusively affects artists who are not working in the pop field. However, there are pop artists who are highly accomplished songwriters, as Stephen Budd of SBM, an elite songwriters' management company, suggests.

There will always be a market for pop artists who just sing, but the ones that can sustain themselves over a lengthy career are the ones that can actually write songs. You only have to look at boy bands over the last ten years. Robbie Williams turned into a very good songwriter and that has moved his career on immeasurably. If he had chosen to rely on other people's songs, then I doubt he'd be anywhere near the position he's in today. Ronan Keating has been relying on other people's material, but is also now starting to develop quite a writing pedigree himself – he's been putting himself in environments with some of the world's biggest songwriters, learning, gaining a lot of knowledge and moving himself towards a long-term career.

So how should you go about writing your first song? Writing is like performing: both are skills you may be lucky enough to be born with or a craft that you can spend your entire life refining. Listen to your favourite songs, work out the chord sequences on your guitar or keyboard if you have one, or study the vocal phrasing. Can you do something similar that is your own? Try putting a different tune over the chord sequence of a melody you've heard elsewhere. These are all exercises in composition, where you mix style and formats in a way that helps you find your own voice as a songwriter. There are also many good books on the market to help you learn to write songs. Get them; read them; learn from them – then put them away, out of sight, and do your own thing.

If you've decided, however, that you don't wish to read music or play an instrument, this doesn't necessarily preclude you from writing songs. Even at the world-class level at which Oskar Paul works, this is not unknown.

I've worked with quite a few great songwriters who can't actually read music or play any instruments, and by that I am talking about *big* names. What they can do, however, is sing a melody to you that is all in their head. Working together with me, we can then capture a fabulous song.

Korda Marshall signed Take That when he was at RCA Records in the early 1990s and that huge boy band are a great example of how having quality original material in your act can get you noticed.

They'd managed to get a three-track demo to me, which had two obvious hits already on there, namely 'Take That And Party' and 'A Million Love Songs'. This was part of Gary Barlow's bedroom demos, recorded on a simple eight-track home-studio machine – nothing more advanced than that. Although very sketchy and rough in some ways, the songs were first-class. 'A Million Love Songs' especially stood out as a very special track.

The fact that Gary Barlow was so obviously a quality songwriter was one of the key reasons that I was so interested in Take That. People say pop acts shouldn't write their own material, but that was a large part of their attraction for me. It subverted the norm. We'd found this slightly podgy and nervous character who was writing these amazing songs. We put him in with other songwriters and producers and nurtured that, but in the first instance that was hugely appealing.

Later, Barlow's songwriting gift became something of a millstone. The burden of expectation on him after Take That split was tangibly suffocating as he struggled to live up to the mantle of 'the next Elton John'. So it can be a double-edged sword, although it has to be said that Barlow has since established himself behind the scenes as a professional songwriter of some repute.

Nonetheless, anyone in the industry will be impressed if you have your own portfolio of songs. There is a key material motivation for writing your own material too, as well as the obvious creative benefits. Put bluntly, the more you record other people's material the more you will have to give away a share of the earnings to that person. In your early days as a performer, you may be tempted to cover some songs by artists you admire. However, when you start working professionally as a recording artist and all your royalties are zooming across into the bank accounts of pop millionaires, you might not admire them quite as much! (See Chapter 11 for more on publishing.)

Try to think long term if you are aiming to write your own material in the pop world. You may do well with your own original songs in a pop act – although this is still the exception, not the rule – but, after the demise of that career, songwriting may be a viable alternative for a strong secondary vocation.

SONGWRITING AS A CAREER

If you realise that you get a bigger buzz from finishing an original composition than you do from performing in front of a crowd, then maybe a career as a songwriter in its own right could be an option. Oskar Paul can strongly recommend this.

> I love what I do and I am lucky to be able to make a living from this, because music is my hobby, too. It's my life. It's great to start early in the morning with nothing but a blank page and by the end of the day have a great song. It's such a rewarding job.

Oskar advises, though, that you need to be aware of what's involved.

> Although it sounds like a glamorous job, the work required is very difficult. I was lucky enough to realise when I was young that I didn't have a good enough voice to be in a band (although I had a very short career when I was fifteen!). In the beginning it will be hard because you need quite a few songs behind you to build up a reputation and you are not receiving any income while you're doing this. So the sooner you start writing and practising, even if you are still at school, the better.

You don't need to be a former chart star such as Gary Barlow, Nik Kershaw or Cathy Dennis to go on to a songwriting career. The songwriters' manager Stephen Budd receives tapes from unknown aspiring writers, but he too is keen to emphasise that this is not an easy career choice. 'You should be honing your craft,' advises Stephen, 'which is something that takes time.' He continues,

> There are very few people who are great songwriters just out of the box. It's a long, hard slog. This means going out there hustling themselves, getting lucky, putting their own projects together, trying to be a part of the music business by meeting as many people as possible, putting themselves into situations where something could develop. It is the numbers game. It is no good sending me a few lyrics on a handwritten piece of paper saying, 'I'm a great lyricist, help me.' That's just going straight into the bin.

Another potential obstacle to bear in mind is that professional songwriting is not a field with regular and numerous vacancies. Stephen Budd suggests there are probably only a few dozen elite writers in the country.

It's a very small clique: there are probably a hundred and fifty to two hundred people signed to major or large independent publishers in the UK who are jobbing songwriters. Of that lot, fifty would be the ones that people get to hear about, and, of that fifty, there are ten to fifteen in high demand, and those are the ones that all the top acts want.

Also, don't use the fact that you have a personality bypass as a reason to be a songwriter rather than a pop star.

From my perspective as a manager of songwriters [says Stephen Budd], there is no point trying to be a songwriter if you haven't got a good personality. I look for someone who can really *sell* themselves. I know songwriters who are just OK, not amazing, but they have the ability to really sell themselves and communicate. Conversely, I know a lot of songwriters who have weak personalities and are not good at communicating, even though they're very talented. And guess what: nothing happens. So if you are a shy, sensitive genius, then perhaps you might be better sticking to being an artist.

One way for an unknown songwriter to try to get in the door is to approach managers of artists directly – perhaps not the major ones, but down the scale a little with a view to suggesting co-writing. This is an approach that can serve you well long into your writing career. 'The American songwriter Rick Knowles has sold phenomenal amounts of records working with English artists,' reveals Stephen. 'He is just relentless, and never gives up.'

You can also co-write with more established songwriters. Despite his lofty status as one of the music industry's most sought-after songsmiths, Oskar Paul is not averse to working with complete unknowns. 'I often work with unsigned people, sometimes as much as fifty per cent of the time,' he says. 'It keeps you interested and helps you find new people and fresh ideas.'

Songwriting success is not just a matter of being able to strum a guitar and write down a few lyrics. 'There aren't so many pure songwriters these days,' explains Stephen. 'They tend to be writers/producers combined. They'll come up with the idea for the track, suggest production ideas and then have the studio skills to take that through to a completed track.' Stephen recommends looking around at some of the production courses on offer, but has a word of warning:

Be aware: there are some dodgy courses out there. If you are serious about becoming a songwriter and are music-based as opposed to just lyric-based, you should be learning about production techniques and how to put demos together. A songwriter's product is the demo, and that has to be of as good quality as possible.

It's worth adding, as a footnote to this chapter, that any professional songwriter first needs to be to get a reputable publishing deal. You'll see more on this in Chapter 11.

4. PLAYING LIVE AND GAINING MORE EXPERIENCE

'I've learned something from every show. There is no substitution for getting a bottle in the head at the wrong angle and having to keep singing.' – Adam Ant

Obviously, how you get more live experience will depend on whether you are a solo performer or in an act. Either way, rehearsals and practice are paramount. For a solo star in the making, Dan Frampton, an engineer who has worked with Liberty X, Ronan Keating and Atomic Kitten among others, suggest self-taping.

Put on a CD by your favourite artist, then really listen. By that I mean not just listening to learn the words and sing along, but listen to how people are phrasing words, their dynamics, every little nuance. Tape yourself. When you think you are crooning like Enrique, listen back and you'll probably discover you actually sound like a wounded cat. It gives you that slice of reality.

(On the subject of self-taping, see also Carrie Grant's comments in Chapter 2.)

REHEARSALS
If you are a pop or rock act, the only way to gain more experience other than performing actual shows is to rehearse. Andy Franks toured the world many times over with Depeche Mode before he became Robbie Williams's tour manager. He cannot emphasise enough the importance of rehearsal.

If you are an electronic band, rehearse in someone's bedroom with your headphones on. If you are a guitar band, find a garage or somewhere that the neighbours aren't going to complain – just *find* somewhere, anywhere! Sometimes, rather than doing five nights rehearsal in a front room, maybe rent a professional rehearsal studio out for a day. In those places you can make more noise. If you've only ever practised in your bedroom and then go out on stage, it's going to be exponentially louder and suddenly you are in this massive hall and you won't be prepared for it. So always rehearse hard, but at the same time know that actual live shows are the best way to practise.

Andy also suggests close analysis of both rehearsals and actual shows.

Even major bands take things for granted. Always try to improve and make it better. Tape your shows and listen back. Constantly try to criticise yourself, maybe even video your performance and watch it back. Depeche Mode often used to watch videos immediately after a show. Remember, you are the only person who can't see the performance.

GETTING YOUR FIRST SHOWS – THE LIONS' DEN
You've sung in your bedroom, you've conquered the local karaoke bar and you may even have been declared the best band ever to play in an empty room of your local pub. It is time to enter the lions' den.

Soliciting your first shows may come before you record a demo, or it may be the other way around. There is an element of chicken and egg here – you may not be able to get some live shows without a good demo; conversely, if you haven't sung anywhere except in the shower, you are probably far short of being able to capture a convincing demo.

However, there are many venues and pubs or clubs that will put you on without a demo or perhaps by just hearing you sing or play. Before you jump on the train to London to play all those concerts in halls filled with chequebook-waving A & R (artists-and-repertoire) people, step back and look at your local scene first.

Even if you live in a tiny village or suburban satellite, there will be a nearby town or city with a modicum of a music scene. Flick through the local papers: there is usually a music page written by very proactive journalists who love to champion local talent. They will feature a band or singer and mention the venues where they are playing. Maybe even phone the writer and ask for his or her advice – and, if that's helpful, keep in touch. Look through local entertainment guides for other venues; go to shows if you are old enough – just do your research.

Assuming you don't need a demo (or have jumped a few pages and have recorded your demo!), how do you go about securing your first shows? Go and meet the venue owner or booker/promoter (at a local level they are often the same person). Tell them you want a gig and, most importantly, how many people you can bring to the show. At this level, their main concern is to get paying punters – and at older venues drinkers – through the door. If you have to be economical with the truth, so be it – but bear in mind that, if you promise 350 people on a Tuesday night and only your aunt turns up, you probably won't be appearing at that club again!

Nigel Hassler is a top agent at Helter Skelter, who book shows for acts such as Eminem, Craig David, Dido and Natalie Imbruglia. 'Some venues will give you a book of tickets and will tick off each person as they come through the door,' he says. 'At first the venue will most likely just use that as a gauge for who to rebook. Once you've played a few times, go back to the pub promoter and maybe they will give you a cut of the door take.'

Many acts can make good money in that way once they develop a following. 'If you have a local pub with four or five hundred people in it,' explains Andy Franks, 'you could make quite a bit of money out of it.'

Get to know the local venue promoters. Don't behave like a superstar when you play there. These people have jobs to do and, if you make their job easier or more enjoyable, you are far more likely to get another booking. Paul Hutton works at Metropolis, one of the music industry's premier promoters. He has some direct advice for nurturing a relationship with a promoter.

It's worth contacting all promoters. Send them demos. I get tons of those. You will have much more chance of getting feedback with local ones, of course, but you never know your luck with the national companies. Sometimes I might book a local act to play with a bigger band because they can bring in an audience in that area. Having said that, don't be too pushy. If you do persuade your local booker to put you in, make extra sure your live show is ready – he won't take that chance again if you sound awful.

The same applies if you've somehow twisted the arm of a few record companies to come and see your show. If you are not ready, you've blown it. I first saw Blur very early on in their career. Everyone was saying how good they were so I went to see them. They were brilliant.

Many bands have worked their local scenes to brilliant effect – even if you are a solo performer, you can learn from their hard graft. As Nigel Hassler recalls,

The Stone Roses built up a great Manchester fan base from playing scores of local live shows and suddenly the press wanted to know what was going on. We heard there was this band who no one had heard of in London, but they were playing to nearly a thousand people in Manchester. It spread from there very quickly after that.

Stereophonics also played scores of gigs around their hometown in Wales and in the process became a very polished and dynamic live proposition. Julian Carrera of their press office, Hall Or Nothing, explains,

Stereophonics succeeded in a local sense by having a sense of bravado. They conquered the local scene to the point they commanded three hundred people a night in their immediate area. They convinced me they were worth working with because of their fantastic songs, and they were just phenomenal live – they had done so much live work in Wales.

They never expected success to come to them, so they worked severely hard, taking a lot of knocks, and just kept persevering such that at a very young age they already had a wealth of live experience. Playing pubs and clubs in South Wales is not the easy option. That powerful, emotive live ability was vital and that comes with time.

ON THE NIGHT OF THE SHOW

Andy Franks advises you to be prepared for every eventuality.

Hire or loan the PA. Because you can't afford to take your own, you normally just have to use what is there. Even then, be aware, you could still get stitched up. The venue might have a 24-channel sound desk but only three channels which work. They might only have one microphone with a short lead and all this sort of crap, so it is vital to have as much advance planning as you can – go down to the venue beforehand, have a thorough sound check and spend as much time as you can making sure that you are happy. Put stuff on the stage, maybe a backdrop with your name on, so people know who you are.

It sounds like a simple mistake, but there's no point doing a blistering gig if the audience don't even know your name.

Nik Moore of Work Hard PR is a top music-business publicist and he recommends that, 'even if there are only six people in the audience, play like your life depends on it', and he adds, 'You don't know who is there and, worse-case scenario, it is a great rehearsal.'

Stephen Barnes offers this specific tip:

Playing live, you should do six songs. Think about your best songs, but it is unlikely that you will have ninety minutes of classic originals just yet. It's much better to leave the stage with the audience gagging for more than boring them to tears after an initially good start.

BATTLE OF THE BANDS/TALENT SHOWS

These can be excellent opportunities to earn live experience (for more on auditions see Chapter 5). You lose nothing by entering, but don't treat them any less seriously just because they are at your local community centre in front of a hundred people. Louis Walsh recommends them highly. 'Talent shows are a great start for bands and pop hopefuls – they give you *confidence*,' he asserts. 'Young bands and acts need confidence and the only way to get that is by performing live, so talent shows should be part of that process.'

As ever, be prepared. 'I get asked to judge talent contests quite often,' says Nik Moore, adding,

There is no harm in talent shows and battles of the bands: you get a gig, there are young people and there is always a chance that local industry people will be there. Often local promoters and agents are scouts for record labels, so who knows what might happen? Remember this, though: make sure you have some CDs, some press releases, contact info, pictures, anything! Maybe even try to sell a few CDs at the back of the hall, but at least have some. It is such a basic idea, but I go to so many talent shows where the winners don't have anything with them at all.

Apart from losing a possible vital contact, what does that say about your professionalism?

When you've just dodged the last flying pasty of the night, or you are trying to explain to a tramp why you would rather he didn't urinate all over your Marshall amp at three in the morning in a city backstreet, then you know you are starting to earn some live experience. It may not sound like much fun, but it is your apprenticeship. Louis Walsh says this is absolutely vital to your having any chance of becoming a pop star. 'Support anyone you can, gig in front of anyone you can, sing anywhere you can, even if at times it's something you're not sure is quite right. Just sing, whether it's a little cabaret club or pub, a party, karaoke, whatever!'

The first time your microphone dies in the middle of a song, you will want the floor to open up and swallow you whole. It is only a matter of time before the guitarist gets so carried away he ends up playing the wrong solo on the wrong song. A drummer *will* drop his sticks and be unable to grasp a replacement, so your energised thrash classic will sound more like an army marching band. You will lose count of the times that you think your voice sounds perfect but the audience look as if they are about to have a stroke – your monitors are obviously well mixed but the sound 'out front' may be painful.

My own punk band, the Chocolate Speedway Riders, became so used to playing in what are affectionately known as 'toilets' that we were unflinching when almost anything went wrong. On one occasion, we played a pub in Cradley Heath in the West Midlands. On our arrival, the pub manager decided this was the time to tell us it was a blues pub and the regulars would expect two 45-minute sets of blues standards. On telling him that we only had eight sub-three-minute punk originals, I thought our lives might be in genuine danger. Yet we played the gig and survived intact. Halfway through, one regular walked up to the stage, gently moved the floor tom to one side mid-song, and walked through a door we were standing in front of – to the gents' loo. Without pausing one beat, we finished the song, making extra room for the now relieved regular to make his way out of the toilet, replace the floor tom and retake his seat with his mate and continue his game of dominoes. We never even blinked. They hated us and our music, but we never even blinked. The only problem was that the Chocolate Speedway Riders' live career path consisted of moving up from tiny toilet venues to not-so-tiny toilets. You might want to go a bit further than that.

One aspect of playing live that you need to be aware of is so-called 'pay-to-play'. Nigel Hassler offers this advice:

If you are asked to make 'a contribution' to allegedly cover the costs of the PA or show, you need to be wary. The venue argue they are providing a proper platform for unknown performers and offering a decent PA and so on, but that is tenuous. Pay-to-play is dying out but at certain venues you can't avoid it. In my opinion it is the less reputable venues which still do that.

The Musicians' Union advises that, if you have managed to negotiate a fee for a gig, find out *in advance* of the show how much you'll be paid, by what means and look out for 'hidden' deductions such as publicity costs or the cost of lighting.

What about getting a support slot to a known act and letting them do all the booking and hard work for you? If only it were that easy! Realistically, an unsigned act will find it very difficult to get a high-profile support slot, although it is not unheard of. Again, your network will be invaluable. 'It's very difficult unless you know someone who is in a major band, a friend, record company, promoter, manager,' suggests Andy Franks, adding,

If you keep hassling someone and they like you, then there might be a chance you'd get a support slot and even then it is an unforgiving task. You might be the first band on at the local pub. You'll have no room on the stage, no chance of a sound check, so it can be quite a nerve-racking experience.

DARE TO BE DIFFERENT

Don't be intimidated. Sing on bills that may not seem suited to your style. Support bands or singers who don't sound exactly like you do. It may be hard work and you may even get your fair share of hecklers, but it is time well spent. Be reasonable, though: don't support Napalm Death if you like singing jazz ballads in a cocktail dress, but think laterally about whom you play or sing live with.

This is an approach that you will see at the very highest level. Tony Wadsworth, president of EMI, recalls the time he first heard that Robbie Williams – at the time no more than a former boy-band member – was going to play Glastonbury Festival.

Artists who are special are willing to take what might sometimes seem like kamikaze shots, yet in doing so they change the perception of them such that when you look back, you think, 'Well, actually, there was nothing unusual about that.' When Robbie played Glastonbury, things changed for ever for him after that, because he made it work. But that is with the benefit of hindsight – at the time it was a pretty adventurous move to make.

BE REALISTIC

One such adventurous move that pop hopefuls and many bands make is to play in London. Opinions conflict about local scenes versus the London circuit. There's an old music-business joke that says that record-company talent scouts won't attend any gig north of Camden. It's not all rosy in the capital, either, however. Part of the problem in London is that the availability of gigs has changed in recent years: 'If you have to go into the lions' den and come down to London,' advises Andy Franks, 'it's getting much harder because there are less gigs on. Previously, every pub on every corner had bands on five nights a week – now it's much more difficult.'

Gigs can be very difficult to get. You might find yourself fourth on the bill at 8 p.m. when the club is virtually empty. More to the point, if you don't get any advance interest in the show, the purpose of travelling hundreds of miles and incurring expenses that can run into several hundred pounds is highly questionable. (For more on this problem of securing gigs, see Chapter 9.)

If you do decide to perform in London, how can you maximise the show? David Rowell, head of marketing at Echo Records, has this advice.

Bringing your own crowd is a start. Local support will influence talent scouts. It is a sign that a buzz has been generated, even if it is mostly your mates. We have a network of talent scouts around the country for us, so good record companies will know what is going on nationally – you don't have to just work London.

Conversely, Nik Moore says, 'Don't get a small-town mentality. Selling out your local pub each Friday is a start but it doesn't mean you will do the same in London. So try to strike a balance.'

You will read in this chapter about how to interest record-company talent scouts who might come to your gig, but you might also like to contact journalists (see Chapter 15). The obvious tried and tested methods, such as flyers and stickering (which is illegal, by the way), are used even by big-name acts to get public interest. If you do get anyone from the music business to attend, don't get carried away. The Chocolate Speedway Riders once played a show at the Bull and Gate in Kentish Town, north London. We had worked our way to top of the bill (OK, there was only one other band playing, but we were above them). We saw this as our big chance and worked for weeks promoting the show, phoning record companies, magazines, even Steve Lamacq of BBC Radio 1. We had virtually no responses but kept persevering nonetheless. The night of the show arrived and we sound-checked and prepared ourselves. We were due on stage at 9.30 p.m., but, to our amazement and joy, by about eight o'clock the venue was starting to fill up. Then we started to notice faces, talent scouts, DJs, famous managers, even a smattering of *NME* cover stars. This was it. All our work had finally paid off. The support band went on stage, played their set to rapturous applause, then, almost as their last note rang out, the venue emptied. We were left to play to my brother and two mates.

If you travel to London and somehow manage to persuade talent scouts or music journalists to come to your show, unless you are more than ready you will crash and burn. A crucial mistake for bands and pop performers is to run before you can walk, which takes you right back to working the local scene first. You need to be as advanced as you can before going 'over the top'. If you already have dozens of shows under your belt and are musically polished, then you have half a chance.

Nigel Hassler advises hopefuls to be realistic about coming down to the capital. 'You will need to come down to do business in London and make contacts,' he says, 'but you don't need to live or play in London exclusively. The streets are not paved in gold.'

I know what you're thinking. This live business sounds like a lot of hard work. Why can't I just record a demo, send it off and get signed to a million-pound deal? Well, apart from the fact that you are living in cloud-cuckoo-land, having little or no live experience will prove to be a permanent handicap, whether you are a solo singer or a band.

For many record companies, certainly for most West End musicals and stage productions – in fact almost any area of the music business – live experience will be a key factor in their wanting to work with you. Korda Marshall believes it is essential.

With the reservation that this differs slightly from genre to genre, I wouldn't sign most artists with little or no live experience. For me it is implicit and intrinsic in their succeeding that they are a great live proposition, whether that is as a band or as a solo artist. It solves so many problems for a record company and you have to understand that.

SOME PRACTICALITIES FOR THE LIVE CIRCUIT

SOUND

At any venue, whether you are a solo star or an act, you need to try to control as many aspects of the show as possible. What is not under your control might go wrong. By control, I don't mean strut around diva-like saying, 'Darlings, the cans are too loud!' Just introduce yourself to the people who work there, be friendly, ask them how they work the desk, what sound they put out and so on. Look at it like this: you've rehearsed for months for this show, you know exactly how every note of every song should sound, but the man at the mixing desk will just be eating a sandwich and trying to get through the five acts he has to put on that night before he can go back home.

One simple answer is to phone a friend. Andy Franks was one of the music business's most experienced and sought-after tour managers even before he worked with Robbie Williams. He can vouch for the considerable benefits of having a mate mixing your sound.

In my early twenties, I'd been playing in bands in Bristol myself and one of them, the Wild Beasts, had become quite successful. We were a four-piece, so we used to have to take it in turns to mix the sound, even though none of us had any training. I used to sing backing vocals from a microphone sat at the mixing desk! I was probably louder than the lead singer!

In this way, Andy's band at least always knew that their sound would reflect what they wanted to hear. 'The band are on stage, the audience are "listening" to it but if the engineer controlling it is uninterested or just crap, you can play as well as you want, it doesn't really matter,' he adds. The importance of controlling your live sound is paramount.

EQUIPMENT

Bring spares. Sound-check properly. Don't lark around with your mates. Get the drummer to slip a spare stick on the side of his bass drum. If you play guitar with a plectrum, tape spares to your mike or amp. Be prepared.

Rest assured that, even at the very highest level, live shows present a multitude of problems on a daily basis. Andy Franks has seen years of obstacles and mishaps, many of which could not have been avoided, all of which provide valuable lessons.

> When Depeche Mode played the Rose Bowl in California in front of sixty-eight thousand people, we had these four hydraulic pillars on which you mounted the lighting and stage set. Then the idea was to lift the roof up, and away you went. But the bloody thing wouldn't go up with all the weight! The guy whose idea this was, Chip Monck, was *the* man who built Woodstock – he was *the* man! He was up there trying to get this thing going. He'd lost his voice shouting at the Mexican stage crew and scaffolders. Meanwhile, the next day, you've got sixty-eight thousand people coming to the show.
>
> Three days before that in Phoenix, we were using these Emulators, which at the time were new prototype computerised keyboards. We're playing in the desert in a hundred and ten degrees of heat, so all the hard disks just completely melted. Sure enough, we got it fixed and none of the crowd knew any thing about it.

OK, you might not be about to perform at a football stadium in front of tens of thousands, but Franks's tale shows what a lottery the live arena can be and how being prepared and working through your problems is vital.

KEEPING COSTS DOWN

Once you start touring or playing larger numbers of shows, either as a band or a solo star, you will have to take on certain new challenges. Before a record deal is signed, you should try to hump your own gear, try to keep all costs to an absolute minimum.

Dave Clark of DPC Media looks after global acts such as the Prodigy. He says that the onerous costs of playing live shows can be crippling and advises any aspiring artist to keep a strict financial check on all costs. Being prudent on the road before you sign a record deal is a good habit to get into.

> Some new artists have room service, expensive hotels, huge food bills, they make all sorts of mistakes. They might get lucky and get a support act to a major name, so they stop at the same hotels and use the same transport, but all they are doing is increasing their debt.

One way around this potential problem is to employ an experienced and reputable tour manager. In the case of the Prodigy, John Fairs of TCP manages what is an extremely complicated touring machine.

Remember: this is your business. If you were a carpenter and went to work at a house in the middle of a field, you would take your own sandwiches, not steamed lobster on a bed of charlottes and sautéed potatoes. The reason for that is that a carpenter would be paying for that and it might take him a day's work to make the money back to pay for that lobster. Live shows are the same, except that a carpenter often makes good money while a live band or solo artist very often loses money.

Even if you have signed your first modest record deal, your debut tour might take in venues of only a few hundred capacity. You are not going to get rich from touring. Obviously, artists who headline festivals can make vast sums, but, even then, the costs of staging that live spectacular can be prohibitive. The Rolling Stones often have the biggest-grossing tours in the world but their costs will be phenomenal. They have to ship juggernauts full of equipment, pay top-class tour management, engineers, roadies and other personnel, pay for stage sets, insurance, accommodation and so on.

Clark says that many new artists sorely mistake the financial benefits of live shows in their early career.

> Young artists and bands really just want to play. They want to sing, perform and so on. But it just isn't that simple. Some bands who might play Reading Festival at 1 p.m. may well only be getting a couple of hundred pounds. That will fall way short of their costs of just getting there and stopping in a hotel for the night. Live shows at first have to target a longer-term goal. Later

in your career, this may change and sizeable revenue can be created from live work, but at first view it as a tool for promotion and profile. It is part of your strategy for the longer term. Above all, watch your costs.

Similarly, don't save up for that rusty Transit. Instead, take this advice from Andy Franks:

> It is too expensive to buy and insure. When you are a musician, everything is expensive, and you will find out that, as soon as you disclose what you do, costs will rocket. Most insurance companies will put the phone down on a musician. Rent a van for a couple of weeks' tour, or, if your friend's got a van you can borrow, fair enough.

Andy also advises you to work with friends at this early stage of doing live shows – and not just because that helps keep costs low.

> A lot of the top people in music started out being roadies because they were mates of the band. Music is one of the few professions where you can go in with absolutely nothing and come out a very rich person, by just living by your wits. Besides, learning about jobs like road crewing will give you a flavour of what it is all about. Most people don't know what is done by the lighting guys, the dimmer man and so on, so go down to a gig and see these people. You might even find out that actually you don't want to play in a band after all. It might open up whole avenue for you.

> Even if (oh, if only!) you find yourself supporting a major act at Wembley Arena, you still need to hold back the bubbly. 'Quite often that support band will be getting a hundred and fifty pounds,' explains Dave Clark. 'Some acts will be generous and say, "Let's give them a couple of grand" – but others might even ask *you* for money to support them.'

THE RIGOURS AND RULES OF THE ROAD
We've all heard tour tales about the rigours of the road (get the video *This Is Spinal Tap* for a hilarious crash course). Andy Franks suggests it is all this and more. His own experience of the health costs of such an itinerant lifestyle is a prime example.

In Europe in 1987, I went with Depeche Mode on their 'Music for the Masses' tour. Two weeks in, I was at a gig and felt really strange. People were saying, 'You're looking a bit odd' – but there was work to do: we were having problems with crash barriers so I had to go running off to resolve that. After I'd sorted the problems out, I went and lay on the floor, not feeling good at all. I eventually went to see a doctor but he couldn't suggest anything, so we carried on with the tour.

Over the next four or five days we carried on, partying as you do, drinking heavily and so on, until we got to Berlin, where I went to see a neurologist. He did some tests and then said, 'I think I know what it is – you've had a massive brain haemorrhage.' Even then I tried to carry on working, but the guys in the white coats came out to get me back and said I was so ill that even to get out of bed could have been fatal. I ended up having five and a half hours of brain surgery which left me virtually blind. In the New Year I was back on the road.

For artists or bands not used to being away from home, Andy suggests it can be quite a culture shock.

Think about when people go on holiday. By the end of the second week they want to go home, they're bored, they miss their families. Being away from home for so long is a very disjointed experience. Obviously the lower down the ladder you are, the harder work it is. You are staying in dodgy hotels, sleeping two, three or four in a room. I did a tour with the Bluebells [of 'Young At Heart' fame] and they used to sleep sometimes five or six in a room.

Even some chart acts will share rooms because the management will still be trying to keep costs to a minimum.

You might think that, if you secure a European support tour to some known act for example, a five-star luxury is just around the corner. Think again. Andy says,

You might have to drive quite a few hundred miles every day. You'll be tired and constantly eating junk food. Moving up a rung might involve being given a tenner and told, 'Go and buy a burger.' Don't think that at this level you'll take your own chefs on the road! There's other strains too: living out of a suitcase, getting your washing done when you can't find a launderette, all this kind of stuff.

Andy suggests that you should plot out routes, arrival times and so on.

If you've got a gig in Weymouth and the next day you have a show in Aberdeen, you have probably got to get up at 4 a.m., or, as most acts do, drive overnight when there is less traffic around. Then you arrive in town the next morning, find somewhere to sleep, grab a few hours' kip and then wake up in time for the show.

Maintain some rules of the road. If there are four band members and one of them never gets there on time, the others are waiting around for half an hour night after night, eventually you're not going to get to a show on time.

These practical difficulties of any road lifestyle are severely compounded by the emotional demands, he says.

Being away from home is a big consideration, especially if you've got girlfriends, boyfriends or wives and kids. It is very difficult, not only for you but for the ones left at home. And, as you are away all the time, they start to live their life without you. And when you come back home, it is like you are starting over again.

As a young performer, Andy thinks in an ideal world you wouldn't have a partner. 'Then you don't care,' he says. 'You're out with your mates having a laugh. It can be a great crack.'

5. AUTIONS

5. AUDITIONS

5. AUDITIONS

'Stand on the star. A verse and a chorus.'
TV producers to Pop Idol *wannabes who have queued for eight hours*

'Less than 1 per cent of the people we are about to see actually have any talent.' – Pete Waterman on Episode 1 of Popstars: The Rivals

The television shows *Popstars* and *Pop Idol* changed everything. In particular, the latter has rewritten many of pop's record books. More people voted for Will Young and Gareth Gates than did for the Conservative Party at the 2001 General Election (8.7 million votes). Fifteen million people, that's 60 per cent of the UK viewing audience, tuned in for the finale of the 23-week series that had gripped the nation. The show had become a national obsession and what that should tell you is not that the UK is always looking for the next pop idol, but that competition for that role has never been fiercer (when the Spice Girls' auditions were held, just four hundred turned up, an impressive figure at the time). When Kym Marsh left Hear'Say, more than three thousand people queued in drizzling rain to audition for the chance to replace her in that chart-topping act. *Pop Idol* queues stretched to ten thousand.

Pete Waterman said that shows like *Pop Idol* and *Popstars* were 'the cheapest and most brutal way of finding out that you are no good'. Similarly, Simon Cowell may have been demonised by the media, but he is a perfect example of the kinds of brutal opinions that knowledgeable people will give you. His portfolio of successes speaks for itself – Westlife need no introduction – so, even if you disagree when he says you are not good enough, you have to ask why he is saying that. Don't burst into tears. This is a business. You will hear things you don't like. Sometimes more often than not.

Some music-industry insiders have criticised these shows for destroying the mystique of finding talent, but this is nonsense. Carrie Grant was the show's vocal coach along with her husband David. She believes that *Pop Idol* cleverly subverted the previously nepotistic music industry.

It is really wrong to criticise *Pop Idol*. For years we've said that success is all about who you know, patting each other on the back and using contacts. Then along comes this show that gets people off the street and says, 'Come and have a go,' and they become huge stars. Then we say, 'Oh! It is so manufactured.' Actually it is the exact opposite of being manufactured: it is just giving the talent the chance to be seen.

This is true – these shows take the A & R out of the music business altogether and gave it to the people.

With this in mind, you need to know that these auditions are a wonderful opportunity for you. You've even got the luxury of being able to watch previous series and learn from others' mistakes. You are very lucky. It might not feel like that at 7 a.m. when you are standing behind four thousand other people, but you are lucky.

Of course, these high-profile shows are not a new concept: they are simply the most extreme commercial manifestation of a process that has helped select pop bands for years. Talent shows have existed for decades and televised talent shows are an age-old small-screen staple. The reason that these more recent shows are so popular is that they represent the modern obsession with celebrity and fame. That generates enormous competition for you, so you had better know what you are doing.

AUDITIONS – WHERE DO I START?

As we've seen, there are often thousands – and almost always hundreds – of applicants for notable auditions. Some aren't half as talented as you and some are twice as good. The people making decisions on whom to sign and record can take in only so much information, and all of them have their own agendas, which can change daily, weekly, monthly and so on. Your job is to make sure that you have given them your very best, and if they turn you down it is not because you failed with your side of the bargain.

Many pop auditions are advertised in trade magazines such as *The Stage*, so that is your first port of call. Finding the auditions is easy enough. The problem is not being useless when you get there. A simple start is to watch every TV audition show, record it, play it back and learn from others' mistakes.

For larger roles or pop acts, you may well have to go through several preliminary auditions before you even get to the main judging panel (see the interview below with Jessica Garlick). Even if you are super-talented, you need to know that the chances are that you will have to be snubbed by more panels than you care to remember.

Don't think that being talented is a licence to be unprepared. You wouldn't go for a job interview not knowing what role they are trying to fill or what type of person they might need. Similarly, don't turn up to an audition and stroll in without being aware of a few basics. Who is behind the audition? What are they looking for? What have they done in the past that might help you? Ready or not, be prepared, because, if you aren't, the other five hundred or five thousand in the queue will be. Find out what they want and give it to them.

Turn up early, get in the queue at the front and settle yourself down. You will be very nervous. Prepare yourself for the harsh lights and barren hall you are entering. Your heart may well be pounding and your hands shaking from nerves. To make your life easier, here are some pointers to help you through the maze of audition clangers.

AUDITION SINS

There are so many 'audition sins' you need to avoid if you are to prevent your life becoming one long slog of never-ending rejections. Here are some of them:

- Don't chew gum.
- Don't wear a football shirt.
- Avoid T-shirts with slogans on them such as that worn by the contestant on *Popstars: The Rivals* whose top pronounced 'Pants' – Pete Waterman had great joy telling him that was exactly what he was.
- Don't wear glasses, even if you need them, but use contacts if possible (so you don't end up singing to the janitor!).
- Take out tongue piercings – they will interfere with your enunciation.
- Switch your mobile off – sounds obvious but it is not unheard of for a searing rendition of 'I Wanna Dance With Somebody' to be interrupted by a bleeping version of the *Mission: Impossible* soundtrack.
- Make eye contact, but don't scare them out of their wits – you are trying to win them over, not stalk them.
- Choose your song wisely – your selection of audition material can say as much about you as the actual performance itself.

On that last point, Louis Walsh says, 'Sing something unusual that will catch my ears: where did I hear that song before?' After a long day listening to dozens of inferior Mariah/Whitney/Ronan copycats, you can earn yourself a head start just by your choice of song. The usual suspects are 'I Will Always Love You', 'The Greatest Love of All', 'Flying Without Wings', 'One Moment in Time', anything by Enrique Iglesias, Mariah, Anastacia, Whitney, Westlife, Ronan, Robbie and so on. You all know the culprits. That panel may have seen hundreds of other people singing that song in the last few hours and they are only human – they get bored, they switch off and, even if you *are* talented, they will barely be listening. You are shooting yourself in the foot. This doesn't mean you should never sing these songs, but maybe a little lateral thinking or alternative selection might help. 'Find obscure Motown songs,' suggests Louis, 'or maybe an old Bob Dylan song. Cat Stevens worked with Westlife. Just find great songs that haven't been flogged to death and give them your own twist.'

Singing a song by a band that a judge already works with is usually a bad idea. If you sing 'Two Become One' in front of Geri Halliwell's producer (or even her), chances are your version will pale by comparison.

It is rarely a good idea to select a song that is predominantly spoken-word or monotone. Even if you are a brilliantly talented vocalist, the panel will not know if you are singing just one note. For example, Shania Twain's interjections on 'That Don't Impress Me Much' worked so well in her super-sexy video set in a hazy desert, with Shania dressed in a size-six leopard-skin cat suit. But that will always sound awful in a cold audition hall. Especially when mumbled by a plumber from Dudley.

Practise your voice, not one particular song. You may be able to sing 'The Greatest Love of All' note perfect, but what if you win through to Round 2 and they dictate which songs you are to perform? Next!

'Make sure that you know the song you have chosen inside out,' advises Sylvia Young. 'If you learned that song from a CD but are planning to use a backing track in the audition, make sure that you rehearse with the backing track, because sometimes the two aren't quite the same.'

It's amazing how many audition hopefuls blindly belt out ballads in front of a panel who are looking for pure pop stars. How many times have you seen Atomic Kitten sing 'One Moment In Time'? If they want a Gareth Gates, don't sing a West End ballad and, if you *are* auditioning for a West End show, a Radiohead B-side is not your best bet.

Watch *Pop Idol* and see how many beautiful and modestly talented girls are rejected after slaughtering a Mariah Carey/Anastacia/Whitney Houston song. It is hard enough standing in a room singing to a panel of strangers, feeling intensely nervous and trying your best to present yourself well. By performing known songs by artists of the calibre of Whitney Houston and her ilk, you are almost always lining yourself up for a very hard fall. We are talking about a tiny elite group of technically meticulous and extraordinarily gifted vocalists. Whitney Houston and Mariah Carey are both rumoured to have five-octave vocal ranges. This is not a talent that you are likely to see at your local karaoke night. This is a rare and special gift. Even Whitney and Mariah are frequently criticised for showcasing their vocal range at the expense of the melody and song, but at least they have the lungs and larynges to cope.

It's important, too, not to warble. But Mariah does, right? Yes, but for a start she has enormous vocal control, acquired over years of singing professionally. Also, most auditions are looking for pop stars part of whose skill is to sing within a group. Solo vocals and group harmonies are two separate challenges. Very few hopefuls can warble with any credibility. Rosie Ribbons is, to my mind, the only girl who ever sang such a song and got away with it. She reduced Pete Waterman to tears with her performance of a Whitney Houston tune, but part of that impact was due to the fact that she made the song her own – she did not imitate. Even then, in later songs for the final, she was chided for overcomplicating her performance. Many pop producers will have an exact idea of how a vocal melody will sound on record and you will required to follow that precisely, so excessive embellishment may put them off very quickly.

In the words of 'Nasty' Nigel Lythgoe, don't 'overegg the pudding'. He used that phrase after the famously bizarre Britney Spears cover by Darius Danesh, but his words sum up a huge problem found at many auditions. People with limited vocal talents walk in and proceed to slaughter what was otherwise a classic song.

Here are some more dos and don'ts under the heading of audition sins (or avoidance of them).

Don't despair

Don't look at stars like Darius and think, 'I can never be that confident.' Just because you cannot 'feel all the love in the room', it doesn't mean you can't be a star.

Don't be something you're not

That is the advice of that songwriter to the stars Oskar Paul. 'I've worked with a lot of very famous artists who are extremely gifted and technical singers, but have no confidence at all,' he says. 'However, sometimes that fragility gives them a unique vulnerability of performance that can be quite amazing. Their voice can touch you in a way that an overconfident voice wouldn't.'

Don't oversell or overkill

Some of the best audition successes are very understated, controlled. So don't shout: sing. 'Don't try too hard,' says Sylvia Young. 'It is difficult to get the balance between being natural and selling your personality.' It seems that, while doing something outrageous in an audition might capture a response, if it doesn't work one hundred per cent of the time, you could end up putting the judge off completely. A gamble you might be better not to take.

Don't copy

Remember, you are an artist in your own right, not an impersonator. We don't need or even want another Ronan Keating or Enrique Iglesias. Copying is always dangerous. Bands who copy Oasis will never be the new Oasis and bands who copy the Spice Girls will never be the new Spice Girls. Fact.

Do be natural

If you come from Bradford, don't sing in an American accent. It is club singing, nothing more. It shows no individuality, no character, no X-factor. Sing in your natural voice.

Don't overstylise

Some people affect their voice so excessively that the panel of judges can't actually make out any words, so dreadful is their enunciation.

Don't try to seduce the panel

Gyrating your butt like a lap dancer is a no-no. If you have natural sex appeal, it will come across without pole dancing around a hyperventilating middle-aged producer. Also, if you are mentally undressing the male judges and ignore any female panellists, how do you think that will make them feel? Ignored? Offended? Damn right.

Nicky Chapman is a good example. On *Popstars* she very quickly saw which girls were right for the band. She had a very acute sense of X-factor and if you overlooked her, forget it.

Do have rhythm

They will want to know if you can dance, or at least show some rhythm, if you are auditioning for a pop (and you invariably will). They won't expect Michael Flatley, but, if you've got two left feet, then some rudimentary dancing lessons might be an idea first. You can always ask at the audition if they expect some dancing with your vocal, but, if they do, don't moonwalk. They are trying to sign a unique talent, not a cliché.

Don't forget body language

Don't move your hands in a club-singer style. If they are watching you on a monitor, don't ignore the camera. Work it. If you are a pop star, you are also a television star – the two are synonymous.

Don't knock the judges

If you're rejected, whatever you do, don't criticise the decision. The judges have a right to dislike your performance and, more importantly, they may well turn up at an audition a few months later. What you don't need is for a judge to remember you only because you told him, 'Take the wax out of your mouldy old ears and check out some real talent!'

Do be prepared

'People come in unprepared, insecure and without any confidence,' sums up Louis Walsh, 'and that puts me off immediately. This is show business, you should come in looking good, dressed well and singing a song that suits you. You can almost see those who have got it right as soon as they walk through the door.'

Don't lose heart

When you are trawling what might seem like an endless round of audition rejections, just remain resolute. There is a method in the madness. Two fourteen-year-old high school students, AJ McLean and Howie Dorough, and Nick Carter, a junior high student, were regulars on the audition circuit in Florida, frequently bumping into each other at the many try-outs for shows, musicals and talent competitions.

Howie was taking jazz, tap and ballet classes, AJ was a keen actor while Nick's supportive mother happily drove him to hundreds of auditions over many years of trying. They are better known to us as three-fifths of one of the biggest boy bands of all-time, the Backstreet Boys.

Beyoncé Knowles first met LaTavia Roberson at auditions for a local children's group in 1990. The judging panel looked at 65 girls, but these two budding starlets won over everyone else. Beyoncé's cousin, Kelly Rowland, was also a highly talented youngster so the three girls got together and started singing and writing songs. They were aged only eight and in elementary school. Ten years later, they were Destiny's Child.

If at all possible, never let yourself get demoralised. Dust yourself down and think, 'The next audition will be the one.' It happens.

Do take advice

The best audition advice comes from people who have actually stood in those long queues, waiting for their chance and have grabbed their moment when it finally arrives. Have you have ever thought how useful it would be to sit down with one of the *Pop Idol* finalists and chat about how they prepared themselves, what it was like, what advice they have? I thought so. That's why I spoke to Jessica Garlick, who made it through to the live final of *Pop Idol* and went on to represent the UK at the Eurovision Song Contest. This is how our conversation went.

MR: Before *Pop Idol* what had you been doing to try to make your way into the music biz?

JG: A million auditions! Always back and forth to London for auditions and lots of different shows. I was working the circuit and hoping someone would be watching. I did Jane McDonald's *Star For a Night* and got through to the final. It was a fantastic thing to do. I also got on to shows like Michael Barrymoore's *My Kind of Music*. I've done a lot of Welsh TV shows as well. I even did a *Crime Watch UK* reconstruction!

MR: So how do you get on to these TV shows? Does it say in the advert it is for a certain TV show?

You scour *The Stage* and other similar magazines to find the auditions. It will say, '*Star For a Night* auditions' or whatever but quite often they would only take the first one hundred that turned up. My first audition I was number 98, so I was very lucky! But I was always first in line at Pineapple Studios in Covent Garden, where they had a lot of auditions. If the audition started at half past ten I was always there for seven o'clock, to make sure I was first in line. That's the way you have to do it. It's hard work. I tried and tried and tried.

MR: What was your experience of singing live the very first time?

JG: When I was three years old, that was my first stage performance. I got to my nursery school and they invited me to perform at the Christmas concert. The main thing I remember was the applause and being dragged off the stage because I wanted to stay there! Ever since then I've sung. I've always been doing something: singing, dancing, acting. At three years old, how can you make your career decision? But I did, I really did. I remember coming out and saying to my mum, 'Mum, I'm going to be a pop star!' and she said, 'OK, darling, if that's what you want to do, then that's what we'll do.' She supported me all the way through, she really believed that's what I wanted to do.

MR: Did you go to stage school?

JG: No, I went to an ordinary school. There was no way we could have afforded for me to go to a stage school. At the time I was one of five children (I'm one of six now), so there was no way. My school was very supportive, though: there were always competitions they would put me forward for. I always had the lead roles in school productions, which was really good for me too. There were competitions every year, some held in theatres as well, and that was my only way of being able to get myself out there. You shouldn't let yourself be intimidated if other hopefuls at the audition are from stage school, those places are fantastic for sure but you have got to believe I yourself.

MR: So you were very dedicated even at school?

JG: Yes – always. It has always been my ambition, it has always been my life goal. And I'm still trying to achieve it and I'm very proud of how far I've got so far, but I think it has only made me hungry for more.

MR: So how did you start to work as a singer?

JG: When I was fifteen, a lady who ran an agency spotted me via a friend. She put jobs my way and I got involved with modelling, too, which was great fun. I'm grateful to people like that who saw that I had something. I worked paper rounds to pay for my backing tracks. It was a very serious thing for me.

MR: How do you get your backing tracks organised?

JG: There are companies out there that sell those. It was difficult at first not knowing where, but it was through a friend of my mum's, who was singing on the clubs, who knew a guy who made backing tracks. There are also catalogues around from which you can order your tracks. Karaoke CDs are always the cheapest way of doing it: you get fifteen songs on there for £10 or so. Or you can buy a single – a lot of the time they will put the backing track on there.

MR: What happened next?

JG: I was singing all the time, wherever and whenever I could. I have always worked on the assumption that you never know who is around – *you never know*. Looking back, I was already meeting people in the business. I see people I met back then now and say, 'I never knew that's what you did!' I was being introduced to the right people, but I thought that if they wanted me they would just take me on board. I thought I'd done my job singing for them and that was it. I think I expected someone to see me and just take me under their wing and say, 'We're going to make you a star' – but that is really not how it works. With age I've grown and realised it doesn't work like that: you *do* have to get out there and knock on doors. You've got to make sure you get noticed.

MR: When did the momentum start to build?

JG: At sixteen I started coming to London and being really serious, going to auditions and trying to get noticed there. I also attended a sixth-form college where I studied performing arts for two years, but I still worked as a singer too, doing the clubs when I could as a part-time job while I was in college. I worked in a bakery too – anything I could, just to get the money to travel to auditions and to buy my backing tracks.

MR: Isn't that an arduous lifestyle for a young hopeful, though?

JG: I did the clubs and pubs for four years. That was my way of getting experience and I think it is an amazing thing for anybody to do. Get into the clubs, get your experience, learn to work with people – that is the key thing. You've got to be comfortable in front of people like you are performing to your family or your mum.

MR: How did you get on to *Pop Idol*?

JG: You have to apply by filling in a big questionnaire. They want to know all sorts of things about you. Then you're given a time to turn up and you think it's just going to be you, but you turn up and they've sectioned it off to take three hundred people at one time! I was one of the first there, sixth in the queue, and I was thinking, 'Why are all these people here? This is *my* slot!' Then you get given numbers and are waiting for two hours before you even get to see the producers. Then you have two auditions in front of producers before you get to see the celebrity judges. On that first day you see two producers of the show in a room with cameramen and they decide whether you go through to the next stage. If you're accepted, you see the executive producers, then you finally get to the judges.

MR: Did that long process surprise you?

JG: Yes. I was expecting the judges. The only goal I'd set myself was to sing for Pete Waterman. That was a big, big thing for me and I was absolutely gutted when I realised that he wasn't there. Lots of people were coming out crying having not got through, but I'd heard them warming up and they sounded really good! You're told you're either a yes, so come back next week, a no, so go home, or a maybe, so they'll see you again at the end of the day. I was actually a maybe. I thought, 'What did I do wrong? Why was I a maybe?' These people going through must be absolutely amazing. Out of my three hundred, only eleven got through to the judges.

MR: Do you think some hopefuls are unrealistic about their chances?

JG: Definitely. I know there's a ninety-five-per-cent knock-back. Had they turned me down, I wouldn't have thought, 'I'm not good enough': I would have thought, 'OK, that's your opinion but I will do this.' I've never let rejection faze me. I think that's why I got through *Pop Idol* so strongly, because I always thought no matter what any one says, even if they tell me I'm rubbish, I know it's not true and I believe in myself.

MR: So why do people like myself, utterly tone deaf and as photogenic as a blancmange, get through?

JG: You have to remember, these are entertainment programmes. It's entertaining for the people at home – every one has a good laugh. They show people who are just hilarious. They go in there and have a good time. Why not have a go, because you never know? Look what happened to Caroline Buckley, the 'YMCA girl' – she's had so much work since! She knows now that she's not a singer, but she's a good entertainer!

MR: When do you get to see Simon Cowell, then?

JG: If you get through that first audition with the producers that I mentioned, you are asked to come back in three days. You do that and sing for the executive producers but the shocking part is, if you get through that, you go straight into the queue to see the judges.

MR: What is it like being in the line of fire of Simon Cowell?

JG: I didn't really know who he was. All I knew was that nobody had got through yet on that day, everyone came out crying! I thought to myself, 'What are they doing in there?' They call your name and when the door opens it's this massive room. The right-hand side of it is filled with runners and journalists. You don't know exactly who they are but they've all got clipboards and are busy writing stuff down. Then all they say is, 'Stand on the star. Verse and a chorus.' I never get nervous. I'm lucky with that – I'm a confident performer. But seeing Pete Waterman, I never realised how I'd react. I started to hyperventilate, I had pins and needles up my arms in my legs, my mouth, my tongue – everywhere! I just had to calm down, but as soon as I started singing I was OK.

MR: As well as the voice and the looks, does personality count? Do they talk to every contestant?

JG: I don't know about anyone else, but I stayed in there for about ten minutes, chatting away. They try to make you feel at ease when you go in, although Simon Cowell is a bit blunt to be honest! I'm the sort of person who will try to make light conversation, let them know a little about me. It was my big chance, so there was no way I was walking out of that room without them knowing more about me. I told them about Bananarama being a big deal for me when I was little and stuff like that. After standing in the queue, there was no way on earth I was leaving without giving them a full show – and letting them know how hard I'd worked.

MR: How easy is it to take their criticisms?

JG: Remember you're being filmed. If you snap or start biting back, you'll be made into a comedy show, and no one's going to want to audition you again or work with you. Bite your tongue and ask them why they think that. If they've said you're no good at all, ask them, 'What do you mean?' You need constructive criticism and you have a right to ask. Thankfully, they were all lovely and thought I'd done really well. In fact, they edited out a clip which I wished they'd kept in where Simon Cowell said, 'Jessica, you've got that X-factor we're looking for. You're coming to London . . .'

MR: Are the TV cameras distracting?

JG: Not for me. Some people were a bit unsettled by that, but if you do this job you're going to be in front of cameras, so I wonder about the people who can't cope with it – maybe the job's not for them.

MR: What happened after they had told you that you were through to the final hundred?

JG: You need to be prepared to stay for three days in London, although you could be going home after the first day. They pay for the final hundred to stay in a hotel and have meals too. When you get to the final one hundred from ten thousand, you know the competition is good. I loved meeting people. Other people kept themselves to themselves. Will didn't mix very much for example: he kept himself to himself most of the time. Gareth was quite shy and always had his mom with him. There were quite a few guardians there. I saw Darius and thought he was there as a celebrity to speak to us about how it all turns out if it goes wrong. No one realised he was there for the audition. We never thought he would do that. I admired him so much for coming back and having been portrayed so badly.

MR: Talk me through getting into the last ten and the live finals.

JG: When they said I was in the last ten, I was so shocked I couldn't believe my luck. I was so pleased the viewers at home had accepted and chosen me. They saw what I needed people to see. I was thinking, 'No one's going to notice me.'

MR: How much harder were the live finals?

JG: It's totally live and things can go wrong. I always prayed before I went on stage that I wouldn't fall over! There's no editing, no stopping halfway through to start again – it was much more pressure. I was helped by the fact I'd had so much TV studio experience. I know Rosie and Zoë had never done that before at all. I had my own PA; I knew how to work the sound, what effects I wanted – reverb or whatever; plus, I was very comfortable in front of the cameras. When I walked out for my first performance and saw the audience I was delighted because I thrive on a live show – you bounce off them.

MR: How did you feel when you finally lost out?

JG: It was quite difficult. The other contestants had become like family – you do bond in such an intense environment and you're with each other all the time. You're thrown in there and think, 'This is it, this is it!' Then all of a sudden you're out. I just kept thinking, 'It wasn't my turn.' It's quite difficult doing the ITV2 shows immediately after because you just want to be with your family, but you have to be a pro. I was proud of myself and what I had achieved. I'd been on the most popular TV show for weeks and got voted by the public into the final ten.

MR: So would you recommend auditioning for TV shows like *Pop Idol*?

JG: Yes! It was the most amazing time of my life. I'd been on this show that affected millions and I'd done myself proud. It was just the start for me. I'm so proud that I've achieved my childhood ambitions and I've just got to look for more now and achieve those too.'

NEVER REST ON YOUR LAURELS

Yet Jessica's story didn't end when she was voted off the show. Only a few months later, she was representing the UK at Eurovision, which, despite frequent criticism, has seen the likes of Abba, Cliff Richard and Celine Dion showcased to a global audience of over 600 million. How Jessica came to represent the UK is a good example of the need to maintain persistence and the work ethic even after you've signed your first record deal. Mat Morrisroe, who heads up her projects on a day-to-day basis for the production company she is working for, takes up the story.

> The song that Jessica sang at Eurovision was just floating around as a demo which had been written by an airline pilot from Birmingham. We were asked to help find an artist to sing and a production team to take the demo to the next stage. We were working with David and Carrie Grant, who had been the vocal coaches on *Pop Idol*, on an unrelated project when they mentioned that Jessica had always wanted to get involved in Eurovision.

Jessica first heard about the opportunity late one night at home in bed, but even then her talent had to come up to scratch.

> One night, I got a call from Carrie at 11.30 p.m. I was already asleep. My mom came in and said, 'It's Carrie Grant!' I grabbed the phone and Carrie said, 'Can you just sing me this note?' and she sang this really high-pitched wail down the phone. I wailed it back and she said, 'Right, that's all I need to know. It's for Eurovision, are you interested?' Of course I was, but Carrie just said, 'Anyway, I'll let you go to sleep. I'll speak to you tomorrow' – and put the phone down! I didn't sleep much that night!

'After that it was very swift,' recounts her manager, Mat. 'She came to London, put down her vocal, and it was "Wow!"' He continues,

> Jessica made that further progress with a bit of chance, good timing and her talent – the song needed a phenomenal voice. People can be quite scathing about TV audition shows but whenever I go to see Jessica, her vocal talent never fails to amaze me. When you meet Jessica it's obvious why she did so well in *Pop Idol*. To start with she can really, really sing. She has charisma in bags and is friendly and outgoing too. However, in addition to

all of this, she also has a certain attitude about her and an acutely professional outlook and work ethic. She has a very professional approach to every minute of every day. That makes people want to work with her.

It's amazing how many talented people don't show a willingness to work, even after they have had some success. It sounds obvious but you will have to work incredibly hard throughout your career. For the promotion for a single, you will be getting about four or five hours' sleep a week. Every day you'll be going from radio to TV, print interviews crammed in, rushing around, live PAs, store openings. You'll be up at 4 a.m. and be lucky to be in bed before midnight. If you're not prepared to do that, even when you've already enjoyed some success, just don't bother at all.

Jessica found that, by striving to keep working and learning, she was able to take Eurovision in her stride.

All that work I'd done over the years equipped me very well for Eurovision. There were six thousand people in the audience, tons of media, but I knew I could rely on my experience. I was so pleased to sing there. When I was twelve I set myself four targets. My four ambitions were to sing for Nigel Martin Smith [Take That's ex-manager], which I did on Star For a Night. Then it was to sing for Pete Waterman, which I did on Pop Idol. The next was to represent my country on Eurovision, and the last one was to appear on Top of the Pops singing my own single, and I've done that.

Jessica was not alone in maximising her success on Pop Idol. Darius Danesh is an example that every aspiring singer and performer can learn from, regardless of whether you like his music or not. His drive and ambition are frighteningly relentless. After performing a bizarre rendition of Britney Spears' 'Hit Me Baby . . . One More Time' on the first series of Popstars, Darius became the butt of the nation's jokes. Yet, just one year later, he was perched atop the charts with his self-penned debut single at number one, having kept Ms Spears herself off the top slot. Even Liam Gallagher is a fan.

Darius completely overhauled his look. He toned down the edges of his personality that were blinding people to his core talent. He took all the barbs of the at times vicious press and came back for more. He continued to write his own songs. He stood in those audition queues all over again. When he was rejected by the *Popstars* panel, he said, 'I will have a number-one single as a solo star and I will have a multi-platinum album by the time I'm thirty-five.' I have to admit, at that precise point, I laughed. Who's laughing now?

Before you put Darius's success down to just perseverance, listen to what Carrie Grant has to say about him.

Darius is really interesting. I didn't like his voice to begin with, but then when we did some work with him we discovered this lovely baritone voice in there. He was like, 'Oh is that good?' And we were like, 'Yes!' He wasn't even using that voice, yet it was brilliant. Then he went and used his baritone on the show and everyone loved it. He still had the cheesy thing going on, until one day around the time he was voted off, actually, he came up to me and David with his guitar and said, 'Would you mind listening to some songs of mine?' David and I looked at each other and thought, 'Oh no, we're going to have to say something nice about this.' He played two songs and we couldn't believe it: suddenly we were looking at this amazing songwriter. We'd unfairly thought that someone with that type of personality couldn't be such a good writer, which was so very wrong. Why else would U2's producer, Steve Lillywhite, have signed him?

6. COMPILING YOUR DEMO PACKAGE

'A record studio isn't much different from a factory. It is just a factory for music.' Van Morrison

'You have no idea how much it costs to look this cheap.' Steven Tyler of Aerosmith

You should now be finally ready to enter a studio and record a demo. What is a demo? Simply put, it is a cassette or CD of a selection of tracks, either your own or cover versions, that you feel best showcases your talent. You will usually not be taken seriously as an aspiring artist or band without a demo to give people. This is your calling card, your CV, your sales pitch, your toe in the door.

The two most important golden rules to remember when you are recording your demo are:

1. KEEP IT SHORT
Three songs are enough. Make certain your best effort comes first. With a mountain of tapes to plough through, many industry experts will make a snap decision within a few seconds of hearing a song. Andy Franks, Robbie Williams's tour manager, tells a chilling story about riding home one night with a top record company talent scout.

> He would put a tape on his car stereo, listen to it for five seconds and, if it wasn't any good, he'd just chuck it out the window. It's terrible when you've spent your whole life building your songs up but that's what you are dealing with. You have to be prepared to deal with ruthless people.

So don't send in a C90 cassette with twenty songs on two sides – it will not get heard and is a waste of your time, energy and money. Likewise, don't send in a demo with a list of excuses such as, 'Check out track two because I wasn't entirely happy with the first one.' Don't say, 'My voice is actually much richer than that, but I'd been to a nightclub the day before and was feeling a little bit the worse for wear.' If a music-business expert hears apologies like that, you are finished, dead in the water.

2. PAY ATTENTION TO PRODUCTION QUALITY

You need to be aware that the quality of submissions – be it on CD or tape – that record companies and other industry figures receive is quite often near to that of an actual chart release. I am sometimes given demos by aspiring artists myself. I was once at a friend's wedding when I was given a demo CD by the groom's brother. The band was called Vex Red. When I got home, I played the CD expecting to hear, as so often happens in these instances, a decidedly inferior dirge. In fact, what I had been given was a home-made demo of the very highest quality. When that band eventually signed a major record deal and found themselves being played on MTV with their debut single 'Can't Smile', I was not surprised to hear that the track that was released was almost identical to the demo I had back at home.

This is not an exception. Celine Dion's massive smash single, 'My Heart Will Go On', for the soundtrack of the biggest-grossing film ever, *Titanic*, was actually a demo version recorded by Dion and her husband Rene. U2's 'The Fly' was also a demo tape. Admittedly, it is difficult to compete with the studio wizardry of the world's premier acts, but not impossible. Daniel Bedingfield did just that, with his chart-topping 'Gotta Get Thru This', which was essentially a DIY production. Does your demo have material on it that could be a hit?

Stephen Barnes of Upshot Promotions was signed to a record deal with his own band, Thousand Yard Stare, in the early 1990s. Since then, he has established a reputation as one of the music industry's top promotion experts. In the course of an ordinary week, he receives sackfuls of demos. Take heed of his advice. 'If you've only got one good song, just put that on there.'

He also highlights the issue of the length of songs.

You should already be trying to show you are aware of the marketplace and what is needed for radio – radio edits of big acts are trimmed down to the vital three minutes. It needn't change the music necessarily, but just show awareness. With that in mind, get to the strengths of each song quickly, whether you wrote it yourself or not. Are you the best singer for decades? Is your drummer the next Keith Moon? Are you really melodic? Aggressive? Whatever is your strength, highlight it. Your demo is setting an agenda saying that you actually think about all aspects of your career.

Also, think of it like this: you are asking people to invest vast amounts of money in you. If your demo is already of such a high standard, their job is easier. Conversely, if you appear to need chaperoning all the way, they may not choose you over someone whose demo is as good as ready for release. So no excuses. Make their job easy.

Here are some other tips worth bearing in mind when you are putting your demo together:

- Spending thousands of pounds will not necessarily help you strike gold. If you have only £50 to invest in your ambitions, you need to spend it on the CD. It is no good spending £25 on a photograph that makes you look sexy but when they play the CD their feet curl.
- Style over content is also often a problem. Don't hand in fifteen songs with loads of glossy artwork and plush packaging, but with music that would make your deaf grandmother cringe.
- Don't overproduce the music, but, if it is a pop demo, make sure the vocals are crystal clear.

USING A STUDIO FOR THE FIRST TIME

The process of recording your demo will depend upon your position and aspirations. If you are a solo pop singer, you can buy backing tracks that will allow you to sing over a known tune. The studio engineer will just need to ensure he has captured your voice appropriately. However, be careful that you don't end up sounding like a poor club singer or tribute act. It is probably best to avoid songs by divas such as Mariah Carey (too difficult for all but a few gifted vocalists) and think about the market you are aiming at – don't cover a B-side by an obscure folk singer if you are sending your CD off to Atomic Kitten's manager.

If you are a band or a pop performer working on your own material, the studio work for your demo is equally, if not more, important. Preferably, get them to write down the basic costs so you can avoid hidden extras. There are various record-industry directories that list local studios, and don't forget the plain old *Yellow Pages*. Ideally, a recommendation would be best, but, in the absence of any local tip-offs, call the studio you are thinking of and ask for rates; find out when they can record your demo and if it is possible to cap the costs; explain that you are starting out and money is an issue.

Once you've booked your first studio session, don't think you can roll in on the day and within weeks you will have *Heat* magazine outside your door questioning you about your new album. Studios are expensive places to be and every second counts. Preparation is the key on a practical and artistic level.

Your choice of songs should be absolutely concrete before you enter the studio. Your equipment must be in working order. And bring spares – at £300 an hour, you don't want to have to go home if a string breaks on your guitar. Prepare and use an equipment list.

Think ahead even more than that: visit the day before to find out where it is, where you can park or how near the bus stop is. They will charge you when your allotted slot starts because it is not their fault you were up late watching *When Animals Attack!* on satellite TV.

A cardinal sin that so many pop hopefuls and bands make is turning up with an unrehearsed backing track or half-written song in the mistaken assumption that some 'magic' in the studio will transform their inept mumblings into a chart classic. It won't, not least because the studio engineer has a day's work to get through and other bands and artists to work with. Unless you are very lucky, the guys in the studio won't be in the least interested in you or your dreams. At least *try* to make them enthuse by being professional. If the studio engineer is suitably inclined, you might find taking him your own rough home demo beforehand will make life easier for all parties.

Make sure you have a distinct plan and expectation of what you want from the session. At the same time, don't be afraid to speak your mind (politely) if things aren't going as you planned. Stephen Jones enjoyed a number-three smash single with the song, 'You're Gorgeous' as Babybird, scored eight other top-forty singles and a top-ten album and went on to work in film soundtracks. He encourages aspiring pop stars to speak their minds if their demo session isn't going as planned.

You should try to focus on exactly what you want. In my experience you do have to forcefully say what you want. It's so easy to get sidetracked in studios with gadgets and people trying to drive your idea in some other direction. Remember that studio producers are often failed musicians, desperate to stick some of themselves into a project. Always remember it is your music. It sounds pious but it is true.

Another mistake studio first-timers make is that, once they've recorded their part, they sit around smoking, playing pool, lazing around on the flea-bitten studio sofa and generally soaking up the rock-and-roll atmosphere. Don't. You should be looking at every minute in a studio as a learning experience. Even if you don't play an instrument, ask the engineer questions. Why has he brought the backing track up almost over your voice for the verse? How did he make you sound so good on that chorus? Why did he record drums to a click track but let the guitarist play freely?

This is a perfect place to start learning. If your career is to be as a recording artist, the studio will play a massive part in your life. Get to know it well. However, remember you are trying to be a pop star, not a studio genius. Dan Frampton thinks you should not worry unduly about acquiring extensive of studio equipment and wizardry. 'You won't stop certain people from spending all their money on bits of gear in order to achieve fame,' he says, 'but you don't need to know how to record. It is more important that a singer spends time singing.'

One possible shock you might want to prepare yourself for is just how disappointed you feel with how your voice sounds in the clinical surroundings of a recording studio. Once you are in the studio, that beautiful voice you've convinced yourself you possess will be stripped bare and held up in digital precision for exactly what it is, warts and all. Dan Frampton is a premier studio mixer/engineer who has worked in the studio with the scores of chart acts, including Steps and Westlife, and offers this advice on the subject.

Anyone who walks into the studio for the first time is pretty naïve, even if they've got massive talent. Many pop acts are put together from adverts in magazines such as the *Stage* and have pretty much come straight out of performance schools. A lot of studio work is very live-orientated and I don't think some performance schools get too involved in recording. There is often a lot that goes unnoticed in a school, theatre or club singing environment, but when you put that under the microscope of the studio it can be a different story altogether.

Pop music is *very* exact. Music is much more perfect in its creation in the modern era. Everything is dead in time and precisely in tune, much less forgiving. In a modern studio, vocals tend to be treated more like a MIDI instrument that has been plugged into a computer and it is therefore expected to be as in time and in tune as every other component. There are a select few serious artists who can sing that precisely – Carol Carpenter, Michael Jackson, for example – but the bulk of performers do not possess that high degree of ability.

Pop artists searching for a record deal in the modern era will therefore be expected to be aware of this more demanding studio environment. Pop bands in the 1970s, for example, will have essentially been a live act, whether that was the actual band or session players, but either way the vocalist would sing over a live recording. 'That makes a very different record to sitting down with a computer,' says Frampton, 'programming a drum card, planning in your keyboards and chopping up a series of guitar lines. It is much more of an exact science.'

As a vocal coach, Carrie Grant offers a different perspective. 'Studio wizardry is all very well but you can lose the soul. I would rather hear someone miss a note but give an amazing performance than have every note perfected by a computer. It is all about soul.'

More recently, some of the more progressive studios have begun to offer packages that are specifically designed to assist aspiring pop hopefuls record a quality demo. Perhaps the most successful example of this is the recent chart-topping success of Blazin' Squad. The band's live agent, Richard Smith of Mission Control, picks up the tale.

One of their friends was on work experience in an east London studio that I know quite well. So Blazin' Squad went in there to record a demo. This particular studio, Xplosive, offered a package where for £99 you got a CD with three tracks, a photo, a bio – and it was all looked after for you. These ten lads came marching in and did these garage tracks. There was just something about the way they all gelled and worked together that was just different. It sounded great and at that time garage was very, very big.

I happened to be in the studio one day and the producers were talking about how they had done a white label of this group of ten lads as a result of the demo. I grabbed their demo and played it to Albert [Samuel, So Solid Crew's manager], who became their management. Eight months later they had a record deal and were at number one in the singles charts with their debut, 'Crossroads'. That's £99 well spent!

Xplosive are a fine studio and their package is a genuine brainwave that has already generated one chart-topping act. Unfortunately, not all studios are as sincere, so be careful. As a sage counterpoint to Xplosive's integrity, the songwriter Oskar Paul warns against many of the adverts asking you to send off your songs to be turned into 'hits'.

> Be very careful. I would rather advise kids to see if there are some local people who can help with the demo than just sending it away. A good song is always a good song and the demo doesn't always need to be so brilliant. Just if you can hear the vocals clearly, that is the most important thing because the whole arrangement and production can be taken care of later.

Some stars recommend you get work experience in a studio even before you record your demo, so that you are fully equipped to get the maximum results. Paul Oakenfold is considered by many to be the world's most successful DJ, and has a long and illustrious career working with the likes of U2, Snoop Dogg, Happy Mondays, New Order, the Cure and Massive Attack. His advice is 'to just get your hands dirty' in a studio. This can be a solid introduction into the business: it allows you to meet other artists and you gain a grasp of some technical skills. From there, you may be in an advantaged position to promote your material or artistic career.

Your need for studio knowledge will also depend on your genre. Oskar Paul says,

> If you just want to be singers, then I would say that sort of work experience is not that important. I would suggest it is more important to study music and get singing lessons or learn to play an instrument. However, other types of artist who make more technically based music where it is more about the beats and the technical side, such as dance, could find this approach helpful.

Other stars take this more involved studio approach one step further by not using a studio at all. Recording technology is so advanced that a high-quality home demo is entirely within your grasp if you are so inclined to learn the mechanics of the equipment. Liam Howlett of the Prodigy shook the record industry up with a demo he recorded at a studio called Earthbound – his bedroom. He had been a hip-hop DJ for a couple of years (see Chapter 13) but was moving into creating his own music.

> I worked at a building site one summer and saved up to buy a Roland W30 keyboard. My dad helped me buy it for £900. That felt like a lot of money but it was a big leap forward with technology for me. With the W30 I could sample, sequence whole tracks together and make proper demos of my own material. At that point, it all really started for me.
>
> I stayed in all the time for months, mastering this equipment. At the same time, I started to hear acid house in 1988. I was really into Public Enemy, still doing hip-hop demos, but I was also experimenting with these newer sounds, trying to bring in something to my music. I was going out, taking ecstasy, getting involved in that scene and using that whole experience to inspire me.
>
> I collected together a ten-song demo done in my bedroom on my W30. I had a few tunes released by XK Records in my collection, so I rang them up. The A & R man, Nick Halkes, told me to send it in, but I said, 'No, just give me ten minutes of your time. I want to bring it in.' I drove to XL in a blue Escort with my mates who all had to wait in reception. I played Nick what turned out to be the whole of my first *Android* EP plus 'Charly', one of the first mixes of that tune. A couple of weeks later, he rang me up at work and told me I had a record deal.
>
> I still only had one keyboard, no money, so I did the whole of the first EP on that W30. I borrowed my friend's mixing desk, which only had bass, treble and mid-range. I tried to mix it in my bedroom. Sonically it was rubbish but it had a raw edge to it. Later, I basically recorded almost all of my debut album, *Experience*, on that W30. The single 'Charly' got to number three in the UK charts and that was written entirely and completed on that Roland W30.

Liam has since sold over 30 million records. That is what genuine talent, drive and a home demo can achieve.

As always, there are sometimes differing views on the need to record a demo, particularly for more pure-pop hopefuls. Louis Walsh is bluntly honest in his opinion that it may not be necessary.

If you look good, are ambitious, hard-working and are a good singer, you may not need one because other avenues could open up. You don't have to be a great singer. If you are in a pop band there will be four or five people, so the voices will blend together anyway. You don't have to be the best singer in the world. Look at Boyzone: only two of them sang – Ronan and Stephen. Yet as a band they were great. More than anything else they had tons of personality, and that's what got them to be so big. In that case their personality was their X-factor. They were fun. People always said they were really nice guys. That's why they succeeded.'

IMAGE AND 'THE LOOK'

A consensus you will get from all the experts in this book is that the music on the demo itself is the single most crucial aspect of your campaign to become a pop star. It has to be a given that your voice, your songs or your sound will be *exceptional*. That is a fact. However, it is also a harsh fact of the music biz that the right look is vital, too, particularly in the pop world. This issue famously polarised the *Pop Idol* judges Simon Cowell and Pete Waterman, who rowed angrily over the oversized Rik Waller. How an artist looks has always been a central part of music's appeal, from back in the 1950s, when a kiss curl and a hip swivel were enough to get Elvis the Pelvis censored but simultaneously sent millions of adoring teenagers apoplectic at the same time.

Music and fashion have been intimate bedfellows as long as the pop charts have existed. In more recent times, the increasingly crucial role of television means that pop hopefuls simply cannot afford to neglect their visual side. So, whether you agree with this element of the music business or not, you need to consider your look and image and, once you are happy with your visual presentation, you then need to capture that in a photograph for your demo package.

Maybe you don't need to conjure up or manufacture a look. Many stars with X-factor just walk in off the street and look fantastic. Jill Furmanovsky is one of the world's leading music photographers, having taken pictures of the Jackson 5, Sting, Bono, Johnny Rotten, Jay Kay and Blur – among many others. She says,

With Oasis, most of the photography they use is documentary style because they didn't need anyone to tell them how to dress or look. They already had two very strong focal points in the

Gallagher brothers, so that was how it worked best for them. I had to just give them the extra edge. Oasis would literally turn up in the clothes they were wearing, do the photo shoot, go out and perhaps do a gig. They still do that now, they have that chemistry.

Jill also believes that Oasis play to their strengths when presenting themselves.

The key to that band visually is Liam, not Noel. He sings really well and he is exquisite to look at. As far as I am aware, when he was at school he was strutting around the playground like a rock star. When Liam isn't at a gig Noel can sing in his place very well, but there is so much less to look at.

However, most people are not a natural rock god like Liam Gallagher and do need to put some thought into their image. Cordelia Plunket is one of the world's leading video producers and has worked with a host of superstars with wildly differing images, including S Club 7, Shania Twain and David Bowie. She therefore deals with the visual element of a star's career on a daily basis. Her thoughts on this subject are invaluable. 'You need to project an image that is natural,' she asserts. 'You shouldn't try to become someone else who is already in the public eye because it is just too obvious. There is a fine line to tread between being influenced and just copying.'

By way of example, look at the image of the shock rocker Marilyn Manson, one of the artists Cordelia has worked with extensively. He may not make your style of music but his image is one of the most powerful in the business: *everyone* knows who he is and what he looks like. Cordelia thinks you can learn a lot from his approach.

Manson is one of those super-focused people. From day one, he knew exactly where he was going and had a precise plan. Manson has always had this dark look: he was never wearing bright T-shirts, it was always black. He would often go out without any makeup for sure, but there would always be this dark edge to him. He is a very artistic and creative guy and he knew which visual direction he wanted to go.

Take his use of contact lenses, for example. He's always played around with that. He is keen to experiment, too. One video I did, we had him in a rubber suit, shaved his eyebrows off and put fake stitches where they had been. He was always looking to take his visuals to new levels, right down to his choice of photographers and video directors.

Image is vital to maintaining a pop career but, from your point of view, it is crucial to getting noticed in the first instance. The record companies you are trying to seduce will therefore be looking for something special. 'You have to remember,' Cordelia continues, 'that record labels want characters. At an opposite extreme to Manson, Gareth Gates may not be quite so dark, but he has his spiky hair and the stutter and, rightly or wrongly, that creates an image and affects how people perceive him. He stands out.'

Cordelia also suggests that, if you haven't got the confidence to work on your look yourself, then maybe ask friends and associates to chip in with ideas. Maybe you know a hairdresser who fancies experimenting or a close friend who wants to be a fashion designer. You are a long way from having your own stylist as all the top pop stars do, but it is vital that you embrace the importance of your look from day one.

Even in the pop world, where so much is made of bands being 'manufactured', a self-awareness of your look and vision can only help your cause. 'Record companies love it when a star says, "This is how I want the next record to sound, the artwork to look, the videos to feel,"' says Cordelia. 'They will respect that even before you are signed, although you need to be able to listen and take on board other ideas, so don't be didactic.'

You don't need to have a complete picture of your eight-album career, but you do need to show awareness.

Darius Danesh is a good example of someone who has used image to contrasting effect. In the first series of *Popstars*, Darius wore his hair in a ponytail and had a goatee beard. Coupled with his legendary butchering of Britney Spears's 'Hit Me Baby . . . One More Time', it was a catastrophic package that made him the butt of many tabloid newspapers' jokes. However, when he returned for *Pop Idol*, the ponytail eventually went and so did the beard. Suddenly, you noticed he was actually a good-looking chap and it was easier to look past that cheesy look and see his talent in its own right. He has since been a *Smash Hits* cover star.

Richard Smith of Mission Control is brutally honest in his opinion of the importance of image in the pop business. 'You can have the best record in the world, but if you've got a set of really ugly people on stage no one's going to buy into it,' he says. 'You have to be pleasing to the eye as well as pleasing to the ear. How many mingers do you know that are pop stars?'

By contrast, Hugh Goldsmith, founder and managing director of Innocent Records, home to Blue, Atomic Kitten, Billie Piper and Martine McCutcheon, warns against overemphasising looks.

The bad news, first, is that it does help if you look great. Or if you have an interesting look. I don't want to make people, especially youngsters, feel downhearted about their chances, but the fact is if they are overweight, it might help to do something about it. Get in the gym! However, what *Pop Idol* and those audition shows prove is that not any old Tom, Dick and Harry can get into quality pop groups. They have to have good voices. You simply can't build a group solely out of people that look right, otherwise you get caught out because the media know.

Of course, all these rules are there to be broken. Look at Thom Yorke of Radiohead. He suffered imprecise eye surgery as a child, which left him with a slightly drooping eyelid. Furthermore, his diminutive build and frail childhood constitution made him an extremely unlikely pop icon. Yet those are the very characteristics that make him a unique front man. His look is so central to Radiohead's imagery that they have even used a single shot of his face, close up, for the deeply disturbing yet breathtaking video for their paean to suicide, 'No Surprises'. Radiohead cleverly complemented Yorke's compelling look with artwork that rarely featured the band members themselves, adding to their unconventional aura.

So believe in your own quirks. There are plenty of other examples – Macy Gray has been dubbed 'the bag lady of rock', Meatloaf, and Jarvis Cocker subvert the hunky-pop-star norm and Badly Drawn Boy is hardly someone you would expect to see picking up music awards.

If you are a natural star, you will intuitively have a strong awareness of your image, an asset that Jill Furmanovsky has seen many times during her years of photographing top stars.

I suspect that the artists who need dressing up are not going to have a very long career. That means they haven't thought something through and music is just too competitive for that slack approach. Some bands give the impression of being very natural but are actually very orchestrated. For example, Madness had seven members and I would get considerable acclaim for the famous photos of them in pyramid shapes and walking in a sloping line. But that was all their own idea! They used to tell me off: I'd be shooting them documentary [style] but they would say, 'We're not ready!'

That's indicative of an act who have a very strong idea of their image and presentation and you have got to try to learn from that. You need to somehow make yourself look different from everybody else. You need to make people notice you.

GETTING PHOTOGRAPHED

Assuming you are comfortable with your look, it is time to get yourself photographed. In many instances, if your CD has already tweaked someone's interest, the accompanying photo may well have an important bearing on your chances of success. Stephen Barnes explains why.

The first question is, 'Have you got a demo and is it any good?' The next question every time, without fail, is, 'What do they look like?' The photo should look comfortable. If you've found a spot that's cool, use it; if you're just sitting on a stool, then so be it. Just make sure you're comfortable. Don't force a pose – it will look hopeless.

There are no hard-and-fast rules but, generally, if you are a solo artist, a head-and-shoulders shot will probably suit best; if you are a band it may work better with a waist-level shot. The pop world will be much more used to receiving a head-and-shoulders portrait, so more artistic pictures might be frowned upon but not by everyone. 'The best idea is to get *amazing* pictures,' suggests Louis Walsh. 'A good picture would make me listen to the demo.'

For guitar bands, try to avoid the 'four-blokes-looking-moody-on-a-building-site' cliché – A & R personnel receive hundreds of these shots every day. It is not unheard of for A & R scouts to receive saucy or pornographic Polaroids, which may find a place on their office notice board but not in the charts. So be aware of your market and make sure your press shots are suitable. Stephen Barnes suggests, 'One very easy barometer is: will you be on the cover of your record? Quite often pop acts are, whereas more alternative bands aren't.'

Don't send holiday snaps or pictures of you at a wedding with the corner cut off where your drunken uncle was falling over a bridesmaid. Remember, all aspects of your demo need to reflect your professionalism. If you have any friends with a degree of proficiency in photography they might help you out if you pay their costs and expenses. You shouldn't dismiss paying a local professional photographer but use your loaf. Don't take your death-metal band into the out-of-town shopping mall and ask for the man who is charging £35 for airbrushed family portraits and dog photos.

Jill Furmanovsky suggests there are plenty of options for getting a good picture.

Your mate can help, yes, because digital cameras these days make taking rudimentary pictures quite straightforward. Another good idea is to hook up with a local art school or art student. Look at it from the photographer's point of view. I get bags of letters asking me how to get into rock photography and without exception I advise people to go and find their local band or artist and help them with their careers.

There are a handful of musicians who are good artists but, generally speaking, the most creative and fruitful marriages are the ones where a band or singer has a mate who is already a graphic artist or illustrator or similar. Storm Thorgeson was a school friend of Pink Floyd's Roger Waters and that was the start of an artistic union between his art and their music that, in my opinion, remains almost unsurpassed. Brian Cannon's design work with Oasis was similarly pivotal in that band's career. He was their mate and between them they created a look for Oasis that was superb.

Such relationships between top photographers (or designers) and the stars they work with are often established at a very early stage. Depeche Mode's famous photographic collaborations with Anton Corbijn are a revered union that may be at a level you can, as yet, only dream of. However, it is a concept that you can certainly replicate to good effect. Who knows, if you become the next Oasis or Craig David, your photographer friend from back home might just become the next Jill Furmanovsky.

If you are feeling brave, suggests Jill, you should consider approaching known photographers, provided you are realistic. Top photographers can earn thousands of pounds for a day's shoot, so understand their time constraints, she says.

> I do work with unsigned acts. I like to help them if I enjoy their music. I will give them the same treatment as if I was being highly paid for a big-name band or star. I can't do this too often, obviously, but I do enjoy that. I did three shoots for a band called White Buffalo for instance, whom I'd seen supporting Marillion and really liked.

One suggestion is to check out the *NME* or other music magazines for photographers whose styles you like or maybe look inside the record sleeves of acts that you admire.

Once you have found the photographer you wish to use, try to keep the costs realistic. Under no circumstances spend money on a photograph from funds that have been budgeted for your demo's music. 'It should probably cost a few hundred pounds for a decent shoot with a good photographer,' suggests Jill. 'Five or ten rolls of film, a studio, even with a student, can be that much. Digital would be cheaper; maybe live shots could save on costs too. You just need to call in favours.'

As with the approach to your studio work, once you have gone to the trouble of organising a photographic shoot, maximise the day. Turn up on time. Have your clothes ready. If you wear heavy makeup, do most of it in advance, perhaps checking again once you get in the studio to take into account the effect of the lights. If you have three band members who are drunk every night, make sure one of you is sober and professional, otherwise you have no chance.

'One reason why Oasis are so huge,' reveals Jill, 'is because they had Noel, who had an incredibly professional approach. He'd been a roadie for Inspiral Carpets for some time and he'd learned the ropes – he knew all the things you had to do.'

If you are a solo artist, stay focused on what you want and don't be bullied into something different. 'And always pay for the very best you can afford,' says Jill. 'Maybe swap a photo shoot for some plumbing, gardening, whatever it is you can do, but get the best possible visuals!'

Think very carefully about the style of photography you wish to use. With both the Strokes and Oasis, for example, the use of grainy, black-and-white documentary photographs has given both bands a sense of being classic acts. Or maybe high-gloss colour shots would be more suitable.

Finally, as with every single piece of advice within this book, there are, of course, always exceptions. The Brit Award winners Belle & Sebastian used to send out frequent press photos that were totally unrelated to the people in the band – one such press shot was actually just a photograph of a bicycle. This might appeal to some A & R people if you are a quirky indie band, but, if you want to challenge Will Young for the *Pop Idol* crown, you are unlikely to do yourself any favours by sending in a snap of your BMX.

VIDEOS

How far should you take your visual presentation? A photograph is essential, but how about recording your own video? With the advances in technology that have seen major blockbuster films like *The Blair Witch Project*, surely you can cut an economical promo clip that will help you become a pop star, can't you? Er . . . no.

'Spending too much money on image and presentation is the biggest mistake I see unsigned artists making,' says the acclaimed video producer Cordelia Plunkett, who adds,

> Spending money on a video is the worst extreme of that and is almost always not a good idea. To achieve a video that is even remotely professional is costly: a super-*super*-cheap video would cost at least five thousand pounds. Even then, the problem is that, if that video clip looks below par, it is negatively affecting how you are perceived; it is not giving you a fair chance. Far from helping your cause, it can really put people off. You cannot compete with the £250,000 budgets of the stars. A couple of good head shots can get yourself in the door just as well.

Yes, I hear you say, but if television is so important maybe I could get my break by sending my video off to MTV or The Box. Don't waste your time. You have enough to do trying to become a pop star without chasing dead ends. It is almost universally acknowledged that unless you have top management, big-budget record-company money behind you and a major agent, you will have no chance of getting on MTV. There are rarely any exceptions, but I have managed to find one.

The Essex band Little Joe Zero took the highly unusual step of filming their own promo video and, without bankrupting their parents or robbing a bank, managed to get a high-quality clip that ended up on MTV2. How did they do this? Their lead singer Olly takes up the tale.

We'd made some demos and done the usual stint of passing them around to record companies. With little interest here and there we carried on writing, recording and mailing for a couple of years. We had a few crap offers, one being if we took on a female singer in place of me, we would be paid £40,000 and given a record deal with a major label. We told him to poke it. We've been ripped off left right and centre and have been suckered into many scams. But we've learned so much from all of them.

There was still no credible interest from record companies, so we hooked up with a guy called Mark Munson, who was a pro skateboarder, snowboarder, Airwalk team manager and basically all-round cool dude. More importantly he was a filmmaker and he and his partner Adrian Frearson have a company called Chill Factor. When we approached them about making a music video for us, they both jumped at the chance. We made the video, with them pulling in favours from everywhere. We managed to get the British Airwalk skate team in the video, and the whole thing only cost fifty quid! This was all down to Ade and Mark, really, because they knew we had no money, and they just wanted to do the video as much as us.

From there I rang up and hassled about two hundred people until I got through to the MTV programmer. I told him about the video and he said to send it on. I did just that and about a week later he rang to say it was going on MTV2! As simple as that, really. We then got on to the Extreme channel on Sky Digital through a friend and on there the video has received heavy exposure. Through the airplay on MTV and Extreme, we managed to get into bigger gigs and better venues, after which things seemed to pick up.

A word of caution, though. Little Joe Zero's tale is a genuinely rare feat. They have showed a laudable degree of focus and effort and have complemented that with invaluable outside support. Plus, they are a brilliant band. I would not necessarily advise you to try to simulate their approach, not least because it is actually far harder than they modestly let on. What you should take from their experience is the resolve, the drive and their passion to progress. Without those facets in your basic armoury, any future opportunity to film a video for your major label debut single will never happen.

YOUR BIO AND COVERING LETTER

It is usually wise to include with your CD and photo a bio of yourself or your band, which can also act as the cover letter for the package. Again this will depend on your act, your aims and your style. Keep any letter short and sweet. No one will bother reading three pages: they just haven't got the time. If anything, it suggests you feel you need more than the music on your demo to keep people interested (however, see Chapter 15 to see how Manic Street Preachers used lengthy letters to make their initial impact).

A good idea can be bullet points, even quirky ones, summarising where you are at and where you want to go, what you've done and so on. It sounds obvious, but make sure your contact details are clearly written out. Most A & R people will prefer it if the paper hasn't got remnants of last night's dinner on it. It might be rock 'n' roll to send out a beer-stained Post-it note but it doesn't say much about your professionalism.

WHAT'S MY NAME?

Last, there are two final elements of your demo package you need to think about, both of which are inextricably linked: your name and, if you are so inclined, your logo. Clearly, a logo tends to work best for a pop band, but the former Five star Abs cleverly rebranded himself with a heavily designed logo of his name. Even if you don't intend to use a logo, this section will enlighten you on the importance of getting your 'name' known.

First, your name itself. If you are lucky, you will have been born with a name that works as a pop star. But we are not all called Fab Moretti (drummer with the Strokes). I'm called Martin Roach, a surname that means the filter on a joint in the UK and cockroach in the US. Not good. I am not suggesting that you *have* to change your name and it is certainly not as important as how you look or, more to the point, how you sound. However, it might add that little extra that helps you make your break.

There are countless examples of huge megastars who have opted for name changes. Most obviously Reg Dwight (Elton John) and Harry Webb (Cliff Richard). Conversely, Engelbert Humperdinck chose that bizarre moniker over his birth name of Arnold George Dorsey and, 130 million records later, it has certainly done him no harm. It's the same with bands: a name is a strange thing. So many aspiring acts are told their name is rubbish, but who on earth thought of Take That? What about the Backstreet Boys or Dumpy's Rusty Nuts? The point is, if you are a genuine talent, there is very little likelihood that your name will prevent your success. Once you start to establish your reputation, your name just becomes a sequence of words that people are familiar with. What I'm suggesting is that in the very first instance you have the opportunity to present an entire image, and your own name, or band name, is central to that.

I can speak from personal experience. The name for the band I was in, the Chocolate Speedway Riders, was suggested by our keyboard player. We loved it and proceeded to plaster stickers all over London's Underground, send hundreds of tapes off, have T-shirts printed and perform dozens of gigs with a ten-foot (three-metre) banner announcing that we were 'Chocolate Speedway Riders'. It was only after we had split up and were reminiscing over a pint one night when the keyboard player finally remembered where he had seen that phrase – in an article about gay slang. Only then did we understand why our attempts at becoming the world's first thrash-punk boy band had attracted only a hardcore crowd of leather-clad, middle-aged men with handlebar moustaches and big biceps.

If you want to go for a logo, don't just pick a nice font off your PC and italicise it. Think this through. You are selling yourself, your band, your act. The name and logo will be central to that sale and, if you succeed, you will become a highly marketed brand. It may sound like an unsavoury premise, but it's a cold, hard fact of the music business. Designing a clever logo can help in that process.

Malcolm Garrett is one of the most successful designers in the music business, having worked with Duran Duran and the Buzzcocks. He stresses how any aspiring performer or act should not just flippantly cobble together any old logo.

If it's just a logo fronting a transparent image, people will see through it immediately. Get to your essence, what you are about, first. It will take some soul searching, analysis and perseverance but, if you can do that, people will sense the honesty and passion and you will win. Audiences can smell a charlatan from a mile away.

Malcolm advises that it might not be wise to pay hundreds of pounds for a professional designer to come up with a logo.

Don't assume if you pay good money to a designer that your presentation will necessarily be any better. It has to be one hundred per cent representative of the ethos of the star, the music, the style, the personality. It's easy to make something look pretty but it needs to be much more than that. Try to look at the broader picture, look at how stars are perceived by an audience, look at what people buy, which aspects of the people you like that they're drawn to. Of course, the music can, and does, stand alone but you can help yourself in the long term by developing a strong, considered visual identity. Without that, your career may be very short-lived.

If you do choose to hire a designer, be very careful. I always tried to put myself in the shoes of the band. You should feel that anyone designing your material should feel like an extra member of the band, not someone outside imposing their ideas on you. A great designer works *with* the band not *for* the band.

7. SENDING OUT YOUR DEMO

'I did loads of stupid things, like the way I used to argue with EMI Records. I just look back to the time now and wonder how I would have reacted to some prick coming into my office shouting and kicking things.' Kevin Rowland of Dexy's Midnight Runners

Fame must be just around the corner, right? Time to book that table at the Ivy? And that holiday in Hawaii? You can if you like, but don't put down any non-refundable deposits. If you've got this far without giving up in a hissy fit of impatience, you are doing well. However, you have only just started.

You're now finally ready to think about sending out your demo to the people who stand between you and your dreams. Here, more than ever, you need to be professional, calculated and methodical or else all your efforts will have been completely wasted – by you.

First, then, a few practical tips. Get as many copies of your tape or CD made as your budget allows. Technology now allows CDs to be burned (copied) relatively economically either at home with your own burner or at a local studio. If you intend to send out dozens of CDs, you may wish to club together and buy a communal burner for economies of scale. Be wary, though, because some more economical local companies may be able to produce two hundred CDs for you more cheaply and quickly than you can yourself.

A simple tip: label the actual CD or tape, and not just the case, with your name, address, email address and telephone number. You cannot allow your CD somehow to land in the hands of someone who matters, someone who sees your genius, then loses the demo in a pile of others only for it to be lost for ever, along with your career. There are enough obstacles *outside* your control in this business, so make sure that what you *can* control is *tightly* controlled. No excuses.

Before we start on who you should send your demo to, a word of caution. The chances of your mailing a major record label an unsolicited demo and being signed to a substantial record deal as a result are *almost zero*. A company like Mushroom Records, home to Ash and Muse, receive between 700 and 1,500 demos a month. Imagine, then, what a huge major label will get through the post. You need to be realistic. You also need to be more creative with your use of your demo.

With that reservation firmly in the forefront of your mind, the next step is, who do you send your demo to? Addressing it to 'The Chairman of Sony or His Boss Who Signed George Michael Way Back When' is not your best idea. For a start, don't just target record-company talent scouts, so-called artist-and-repertoire (or A & R) people. True, it is their job to sign new acts and their own career will rise or fall on their selections. However, they are but one cog in the music-business machine. The demo will also play a key role in getting more live experience. So you need to broaden your net and think about venues, bookers, managers, agents and other performers.

Ideally, you will have a few contacts of your own. Maybe a friend of the family works with someone who plays in bands at weekends. This may sound tenuous, but if he plays in bands he may know more about the local scene; he may even put your tape in the hands of an agent or scout. You never know. It is worth the price of a stamp to get a copy to him and a polite phone call to follow up.

Realistically, however, many of you reading this book will know not one solitary person in the music business (apart from yourself). If this is the case, you need a few basic tips to get you started. For one, you need to create your own list of contacts, your database. You can get hold of numerous music-biz directories that list all the record companies and other key personnel in the business (*Music Week Directory*, *The White Book*), and the Internet is also a useful resource tool. However, spending a month's wage mailing out a CD to everyone listed under 'Pop: Record Companies' is not going to get you anywhere. You need to compile a mailing list that is thoroughly researched.

There are three levels to which you need to pitch, and this is a technique that applies to soliciting gigs, record deals, managers and so on. First, your prime targets. Go through the industry books and any contacts you already have with a fine-tooth comb. Who are the record labels that release the kind of music you are making? Where are the venues where you want to sing? What are the shows that bands like yours are playing?

If you can find a phone number, call them up and ask for the name of the person who you should send your demo tape to. You are talking to someone on reception who is probably eating a yoghurt and waiting to be discovered themselves, so don't expect too much. If you are told to send it to a general department, ask politely if there is a specific name they can give you. If you don't get it, don't worry.

When you have been through all the first-choice companies or names, you have your most important list of contacts, your 'top of the bill' if you like. Do exactly the same again with the companies you think *might* be worthwhile, and collate your 'support acts' list. Last, if you are feeling suitably robust, trawl every single opportunity and get the details of every company in the business, good or bad, which to complete the analogy, I will call your 'pub singers' list.

While you are compiling this list, be it on the phone or talking to someone at a show, never *ever* be a snob. Just because you are talking to the A & R man's assistant, don't be a jerk with them – remember, they will/will not put your phone calls through to the person who writes the cheques. You need to assume that everyone you speak to deserves your respect, out of courtesy if nothing else. If you discover they are, in fact, an arsehole (and, believe me, you will meet quite a few), be polite and move on to the next contact. Furthermore, the music business is renowned for promoting from within, so that assistant you were snotty to last year, when your tape was rubbish anyway, might later become head of A & R. Bad move!

Your top-of-the-bill list should not be exclusively major labels and huge names in the business. For a start, these are the contacts that you are least likely to get any feedback from. Darrin Woodford is director of A & R at Echo, a Chrysalis Records label.

> It is easier to access A & R at smaller labels than majors [he says]. Targeting these could be a wise strategy if you are sending demos out. If you sent me something here, it will get listened to and if we like it we will get in touch. It is probably better to assume that a major label simply won't be able to get through all the tapes.

Once you have your contacts list and you are sitting down with the envelopes, make sure they're clearly labelled. Even if you decide that the only way to reflect the ethereal and magical brilliance of your prog-rock vocal is by writing all your letters on cling film, at least address the parcel clearly, preferably using an address label produced by a computer printer. It's no good sitting at home waiting for the phone call from Simon Cowell when in fact a bemused but enthusiastic butcher in Epping has been playing your CD in his car for weeks. Some talent scouts suggest you include a self-addressed envelope with the postage paid for return of your material. Others say they don't have the time to return packages but most will if you include an SAE.

Sometimes a bright package will stand out in the towering pile of wannabe CDs. Other A & R people will ignore such gimmicks altogether. Sometimes sending an 'advance present' can help – to a point. My band once sent a pair of charred Y-front underpants to a prominent A & R person with a note saying, 'Our tape is coming soon and it's so hot it will burn your arse off.' A week later we sent the package with a Polaroid of the burned underpants taped to the front. Sure enough, the A & R man was suitably intrigued and not only opened our parcel and listened to the tape but also phoned us back – all within 48 hours. He said the pants had made him laugh but we were useless.

You should keep diary listings for your work to date. A week after your first mail-out, telephone everyone on your top-of-the-bill list. Ask to speak to them in person and, if they aren't available right away, be patient and polite and ask when it would be convenient to call back. When you finally get through, explain *briefly* who you are and explain that you sent a demo tape and package, and ask if they have had the chance to hear it yet. Make sure you mention your name.

If they tell you that they have and it is not for them, thank them kindly and politely, and ask could they possibly let you have it back using the envelope you provided. Don't ask for advice or try to tell them why they should change their mind – they have heard you, they don't want you, and they have three hundred other things to do that day, so just remain professional and get off their line as quickly as you can. Besides, you have dozens of calls to make yourself, so stop wasting time. If they haven't heard your tape yet, thank them for their time and say you'll look forward to hearing from them. You can then repeat this with the 'supporting acts' and 'pub singers' lists you've compiled, depending on the thickness of your skin and your will to live.

Ultimately, your ability to get your demo into the hands of people who can make a difference is down to you. The A & R veteran Korda Marshall signed Take That from a demo but their management got a tape to him, rather than through a blind mail-out.

I think sending in tapes cold is just no good. Determined artists eventually get through to me somehow. They might stand outside my office all day until I finally surface. They might know someone who sort of knows someone else who is meeting me that evening. You have to think laterally and use any trick or avenue to get that edge. If I just get a tape mailed through from someone I've had no contact with at all, it suggests to me they aren't thinking hard enough. Get out there and network!

If the door's closed, find a key, get around it, under it, over it. One of my talent scouts came in here two years ago and said, 'I just want to work here. I'll clean your ashtrays. In fact, there's one that needs cleaning out now.' He just had this can-do attitude and you should apply the same to your career as an artist. I get hundreds of tapes a month – how can I possibly find yours in there if there is no prior connection?

If you are very lucky, you may persuade an A & R person to come to one of your shows. First tip: resign yourself to the fact that they almost certainly won't turn up. Second tip: learn how to spot them if they do. Stephen Barnes of Upshot Promotions talks about A & R like David Attenborough observing a herd of antelope. He has some wise words for those of you who are on the lookout.

A & R have a certain look! They often have record-company bags, usually look a little detached, like they are not real punters and hang around in packs. One obvious tip: if you somehow manage to persuade one to come to a gig, ask them what they look like. Of course, if they want to sign you they'll make themselves known, but, if they're not so sure, it'll still be very helpful to get their opinion, so grab them before they leave. If you don't make contact on the night, phone them and ask politely. Remember, above all, A & R tend to not listen to tapes: they listen to other people. Their biggest fear is, 'I missed it.' Get the business worried like that and you can't fail.

Here is one final suggestion about sending out your demo. Try known artists. You do, however, need to be realistic. If you tape yourself on your mum's stereo singing 'Candle in the Wind' in the lounge with *Coronation Street* on in the background and send this off to Elton John, you may be waiting quite a while for the phone call!

Paul Oakenfold avidly accepts demos from hopefuls and insists this process is a vital part of the endless cycle of musical progress. 'I get sent loads of tapes and demos,' he says. 'It's great. I encourage people to give me stuff because it is the only way to find new music and new talent.'

Perhaps you could choose an artist who is more accessible than Sir Elton. Go to a show at a smaller venue and try to root out the act's manager. The Strokes threw a tape of their demo on to the stage at a gig by their favourite band, Guided By Voices. The latter played it, loved it and offered the Strokes a support slot. That said, showering artists with CDs is more likely to land you with a lawsuit for eye injury than it is a career breakthrough. Nonetheless, think laterally. How might you get your CD to someone who receives a thousand fan letters a week?

SO YOU ARE IN WITH THE A & R MAN . . .
The unthinkable has happened. The phone has rung or you've received a letter. Someone has actually listened to your CD rather than use the case as a coaster for their 'World's Greatest Farter' mug. They want to meet you. With the reservation that this is about as likely to happen as winning the Lotto two weeks in a row (well, almost), there are some basic rules to follow that will help you present yourself at your very best.

1. Don't panic
2. Stop jumping around the room and sit down
3. Draw yourself up a battle plan

Here are a few pointers to help you. Plan ahead for the day. There may be a thousand reasons why you turn up two hours late, but the record company won't be interested in any of them. If you have to travel five hundred miles to be there, consider travelling a day early and sleep on a friend's floor rather than trust that the train will be on time or the bus won't be held up. This could be the most important thirty minutes of your life, so get there early. If you are there two hours early, wait until five minutes before your appointment, and then let the receptionist know you've arrived.

You may arrive at the record company's reception with great excitement. The foyer will probably be super-plush, there might be a table football in the corner, definitely some trendy sofas and perhaps a huge flat-screen television with MTV playing. Don't be fooled. These are just the necessary trappings of the pop game. Certainly don't be intimidated. All that counts is the CD in your pocket and what the person upstairs thinks of you. It might pay to catch a glimpse of any gold or silver discs that will inevitably be littered on the walls, just to refresh yourself about the company's roster (but you already know this because of the research you did for your database, right?).

The meeting with the A & R is the time when you are on your own. For goodness' sake, make strong and immediate eye contact but don't stare at them as if you were about to chin them. Ordinarily, for any other job interview, you would be advised to dress smart, speak clearly and so on. As this is music, those rules do not always apply. Your presentation at this meeting is the record company's first actual view of you in person, so this is where all that work and thought about your image will pay dividends.

Stephen Barnes suggests that if possible you should not go to the record company's office for the meeting. 'Invite them to a show, put the meeting into your environment if you can,' he says. 'If they're really interested they'll come, and then it's on your terms, in your world, which will make you much less nervous. It's a little trick to help defuse any anxiety you may have.'

If you do invite them to a show, pick one of your better bookings and use every waking second of the days before the performance to make sure the venue is filled to brimming. Pay people, wash cars, beg – whatever it takes.

Whether you meet upstairs at the Dog and Bucket or in the swanky boardroom of a record company office, prepare yourself by thinking about the person you are about to meet. If that A & R works at a major record label, their department will receive several hundreds demos a week. Yet you are someone they have deemed to be worth seeing in person. They will be looking to see if you look as good as your photo suggested, or if you are just very good with Adobe Photoshop. You may be asked you to sing – unusual for rock acts but entirely possible in front of pop talent scouts. If you are, do exactly what they ask, nothing more, nothing less. Listen carefully to what your interviewer tells you, and don't get carried away by the moment and blather on endlessly about how you love Ricky Martin and you are *so* the next Latin love god.

Darrin Woodford says it's important not to be too nervous.

If I really love the music it would actually be quite hard for an artist to put me off in that first meeting. If I felt they were just in it for the deal, seeing who could pay the biggest advance, that would disinterest me, as I am looking for genuine, long-term attitudes. Other than that, you would be hard put to totally turn me off.

Before you go in, tell yourself that even if you fail this is the nearest you have got yet to being a global superstar and know that you will learn more about how to get on to the next step of the ladder in the next thirty minutes than ever before.

Be realistic. It is unlikely, to say the least, that you will walk out of that meeting with any kind of offer, never mind a multimillion-pound one. Indeed, some might suggest that, if you do after just one meeting, alarm bells should perhaps be ringing. It can and does happen, although often this will be after the A & R has already seen you perform live and knows what they are signing in more detail. If nothing comes of the meeting at all, don't despair. It can take years to succeed, but sometimes it can be only a matter of months between an A & R man's hearing your demo and your signing the deal. So stay buoyant. In your darkest hour, you might only be three months from your crowning moment.

If you hit the jackpot and a record deal is offered, take your time. You are better off with no deal than a bad deal, some of which can tie you up for years and years. If you are a pop performer, by the time you extricate yourself from a poor contract, your career could effectively be over (see Chapter 11 for more advice on what to look out for in a record deal). Listen to what the A & R executive is saying, what their projections are for your music. Is this person in tune with your own ideas? By way of example, Kylie Minogue's recent phoenix-like return to form on Parlophone reflects the synergy between what she wanted and what the record company craved: 'I had my slight concerns that we were going to end up with an album slightly to the left of Nick Cave,' explains Tony Wadsworth, president of EMI. He continues,

So when I had my meeting with Kylie I asked her directly, 'What type of album do you want to make?' And she said, 'I just want to make a great-quality pop album.' So at that point I thought, 'Great!' We were all on the same page. I think you need to make sure you all have an understanding from the beginning. If there are very clear gaps in your agreement before you even sign the deal then it is only going to get worse after you have put pen to paper. Don't ever think to yourself, 'I'll just get it signed, then change their mind about me.'

WHY DO A & R SIGN A PARTICULAR ACT?

A & R sign lots of different bands for lots of different reasons. Korda Marshall signed Take That back in 1991 and his reasons are very enlightening for any aspiring pop star to read.

There were three principal reasons that made me want to sign Take That. Firstly, the aforementioned three-track demo [see Chapter 3] that Gary Barlow had recorded. Secondly, they looked fantastic. The photographs were superb, their skin seemed blemish-free, their hair was great, they just had a look. Thirdly, they were excellent dancers. I went to see them at Heaven, the gay [London] nightclub, where they just came on and mimed, but even there they had something. I remember seeing Boyzone on an Irish TV show trying to dance and it was famously bad, but Take That were mostly naturals.

Overlapping all of that was the marketplace at the time. It was three years since Bros had finished; New Kids on the Block were also defunct. So at that specific point in time there were no pure-pop bands. There weren't any bands for girls to scream outside radio stations at. At the time, I was at RCA, which had a strong history of successful pop acts, such as Rick Astley and Five Star. We spotted a gap in the market and Take That fitted that vacuum perfectly. That would be a key point of advice – if you spot something that is not happening, that is absent, then there is every chance it may be about to happen.

If that's how record companies think, then maybe as an artist you can pre-empt that thought process.

Even though it would be unwise to look to the multi-platinum Robbie Williams for parallels for your own unsigned career, Korda does recall certain characteristics that aspiring artists could do well to learn from.

When I first met Robbie Williams, his determination to succeed was fearsome. At all costs, he had a huge drive. He was a great sponge: he soaked everything up that was put forward to him; at that stage he took direction. Robbie was the funny little one. When we first started working with them, it would be me and Robbie going down an alley for a quick cigarette after *Top of the Pops*. He was so full of character even then. He turned the negative things in his life into positives and managed to get material out of them, and that essence of emotional content shines through.

So what should unsigned artists know about a pop label's choice of acts to sign that might help them get to work with people like Hugh Goldsmith of Innocent Records?

We sign the right artists, we sign the right individuals. As an industry we tend to be a little sheeplike in our mentality. There'll be acts that come through and have significant success which then get followed by acts of exactly the same makeup, but none of the pretenders to the throne ever do as well as the original.

Hugh warns that although he works with pop acts, he is always on the lookout for long-term potential.

One swallow a summer doth not make. You need to keep the hits coming to give yourself a chance of selling albums. I would say no artist is immune any longer to the need for a stream of fantastic records. There was a time a few years ago, if you were Madonna or Michael Jackson, when all you had to do was put the record out and you were going to have a big hit. Now I think that, whoever you are, you have to consistently be making quality records.

You are also up against the odds trying to persuade a pop label to take a risk. For pop acts, any new talent that has been heavily funded and promoted at massive cost can sometimes have no more than a one-in-twenty chance of succeeding. In other words, for every band you see on the TV selling records and doing well, there could be up to nineteen others with their dreams in tatters. Others put the figures lower than that, nearer one in thirty. So it is vital you align yourself with a pop label that has good record. Ideally, don't be that company's first foray into what is a specialist field. Take Hugh Goldsmith as an example, the founder and managing director of Innocent Records, home to Atomic Kitten, Blue, Billie Piper and Martine McCutcheon. Hugh's success rate with Innocent is one of the highest in the business, with one in three singles hitting number one. Of the five long-term album deals he has signed, four have gone platinum. So check out the track record of any pop label you are talking to.

The reason I emphasise the need to be professional is that you are asking people like Hugh to make vast investments in you.

These are million-pound mistakes. Every time an act is put into the market by a major it costs about a million pounds. By the time you have made an album for a quarter of a million pounds, made a couple of videos for a hundred thousand pounds each, paid the band an advance, paid the marketing and promotion, this, that and the other, you'll get no change from a million pounds.

So how can you persuade Hugh to pull out a million pounds for your career?

I hate to say it, but it is a combination of look, voice and character. I'm always on the lookout for charismatic people – charismatic because they are funny or because they are bright and they hold your attention But it has to be the entire package. When you're on stage or TV singing live, you have to be able to sing and look great; when you are doing an interview, you have to be able to be interesting in a way that is aspirational to the people you are targeting; when you are in a photo shoot you have to look great.

Hugh has no time for pop wimps. 'If you don't have "bottle", forget it and do something else,' he advises. 'If you can't stand the heat get out of the kitchen. If you can't handle the concept of doing an audition, if you are throwing up and just can't handle it, don't bother. If that's the case, how are you going to be able to handle *Top of the Pops*?'

Hugh prefers to work with pop acts who have musical knowledge. Blue are a case in point.

Blue love music, which is a really important point to make. They are not in it purely to make money and be famous: they are in it because they love music. Every free moment they get they are in the studio. They ring me last thing at night and first thing in the morning saying, 'Just wrote a song last night . . .' and they've been in the studio all night. Some nights it does my head in when it's really late, but I love it. They will call from the studio where they've been all night, then you wake up and see them live on Saturday-morning shows. That is what I want. I want people who have the desire.

Hugh reckons that, 'If you are in it to be famous, then I'm sorry to say you should go and do something else.'

The bottom line, according to Natalie Appleton, is, 'Executives don't care about you personally. It's a working partnership: they want to make money and that is their bottom line.'

THE EVER-CHANGING WORLD OF A & R

The first rule to remember about being spotted is: *there are no rules*. The charts are littered with acts who were turned down a hundred times before going on to change the world. Most famously, Decca turned down the Beatles, but they are not alone: most A & R people have their own horror stories. The wastelands of the 'failed talent scout' are also strewn with 'retired' former executives whose last successful signing was a Lycra-clad, mullet-wearing 1970s sensation (for a week). These people are under immense pressure and there is one dreaded question that is a very brutal barometer of their success: 'So who have you signed, then?'

Darrin Woodford snubs the theory that there are hundreds of unsigned musical prodigies. 'I find it hard to believe that if a band was a truly great band or performer that they would never make it,' he says. 'That doesn't mean it's easy, but talent should always triumph.' Other A & R people go so far as to suggest that they are always struggling to find new stars who are good enough to sign.

However, even allowing for this apparent dearth of new talent, your success, in some respects, is little more than a lottery. The same man who tells you that he isn't interested in R&B singers at the moment because he has the top three in the world already on his books may change his mind next week when two of those stars leave his label. If you are the next Spice Girls and you think that their record company is obviously the one to pursue, don't be surprised if they might actually be looking for a thrash-metal band to eliminate the imbalance of having an excessively pop roster. Yet a month later they might be scouring the audition world for two four-piece girl groups!

THE X-FACTOR

Finally, remember this: despite what you might think, every record company is always keenly looking for real talent and real star quality. The reason so many people are rejected is not that the industry doesn't know a superstar when one stands in front of it, but because the vast majority of wannabes simply do not have 'X-factor'.

So what is X-factor? It is that intangible star quality, charisma, an edge. You hear record companies talking about it is if it were the Holy Grail – and that, metaphorically speaking, is just what it is. When someone walks into a room with a good demo and X-factor, they *will* get signed. In his twenty years in the music business, Tony Wadsworth has come to recognise X-factor like a beacon. Tony is president of EMI and can boast bands such as Atomic Kitten, Blue, Coldplay, Kylie and Robbie Williams on his roster. He feels that you can prepare and plan for the A & R meeting, but, if you don't have an X-factor, you are struggling.

The first time you meet Damon Albarn, you can see a combination of enthusiasm, talent, ambition and energy. Most extremely successful pop stars, rock stars and musicians are different. They have whatever it takes and in spades; plus, they'll have a larger amount of ambition and belief than the average person. Likewise, they are very bright in their own chosen field. People outside of the business might think otherwise, because a lot of these stars try to put that image out, but think about it: anybody who gets to the top of their profession has to have certain qualities that set them apart.

Take Kylie Minogue, for example. There you've got somebody who can light up a room when she wants to, yet can also talk to you one to one as a normal human being. She is quite special in that respect. Plus, when I first met her was definitely a burning ambition still there.

Korda Marshall says,

I have a very old-fashioned gauge of whether someone is a star in the making, has that X-factor. When I see a new act, do the hairs on the back of my arms stand up? I get that tingle when I listen to Beethoven; I get it listening to Radiohead; and I certainly expect to get that from any new artist I am proposing to invest a lot of money and effort into.

Albert Samuel manages So Solid Crew and he could see the X-factor in Megaman straightaway.

Megaman is very charismatic. He has an unshakable belief in his ideas. At the same time, he listens to ideas and input, but his own perception and vision is excellent. That's what separates good artists from great artists, their awareness of where they are currently and where they are going. All the major artists out there have that in common.

If you have the X-factor, you may not even be aware of it. At times, nor will other people. You will still get rejected. This is not a passport to an easy ride. Will Young stewed in the 'maybe room' for a whole day. Darius was flatly rejected for *Popstars* and reached the final ten of *Pop Idol* only because Rik Waller pulled out with a sore throat. They both have X-factor. Do you?

8. THE LOWDOWN ON MANAGERS

'When I first knew Elvis, he had a million dollars' worth of talent. Now he has a million dollars.' Colonel Tom Parker, Elvis Presley's manager

The music business, *your* business, can be a quagmire. Before you are famous, people will not talk to you, phone calls will go unanswered, your demo might sit gathering dust for months before someone will listen to it, you might get promised money for shows and not see a penny. As your career progresses, however, the phone calls will be returned (you will start to get unsolicited calls even), money will start to trickle in, new opportunities will arise. Eventually, it will become necessary to find a manager.

What is a manager? It's a word that's used to cover multiskilled global music-biz experts as well as the mate of the band who was the only one who couldn't play an instrument or sing. A successful and astute artist manager will have to deal with every aspect of your career, including studios, gigs, TV, co-ordinating press, record-company liaison, career strategies . . . The list is endless. Some really huge acts have a manager plus a business manager, because their profile and financial turnover are equivalent to those of a large corporation. Bands such as U2 are among their countries' biggest financial exports. At one point, Abba were worth more to the Swedish economy than Volvo. You can forget about a business manager at this stage, however – that is a long, long way off. Suffice to say, if you are to become a pop star you will need a manager and that person will probably be the single most important figure you work with in your entire career.

So when do you get a manager? A common mistake is to rush into signing one up. It feels good to tell your friends and music-industry people you have one, that you can now concentrate on getting your art perfect, relaxing with your muse and basking in your own genius. Then, when the Swindon Men's Club pay you £30 for the show you did last week, you will have to hand over £6 to your manager. It cost you £26 to get there, eat some food and get home. *You* do the arithmetic!

The point is this: in the early stages of your career, you do not need a manager, says Stephen Barnes.

Young artists think that a manager will take all the hassle out of their career. However, at such an early stage, what exactly is that manager going to do for you that you can't do yourself? All you are doing is playing pseudo-pop-star, which suggests to me you are in it for the wrong reasons, so perhaps you should forget it. My advice would be to hold off for some time, unless you are absolutely certain. Usually, until you are already talking about record contracts, agents and legal stuff, you don't need representation.

SELF-MANAGEMENT

So why not manage yourself? At first, you can and should. It will be a fantastic way to learn about all aspects of the business at grassroots level. It will equip you to understand situations later on when you are more successful. Although this may feel like a burden, it is in fact a vital apprenticeship. Listen to advice, take on jobs or tasks that you know little about and find out more. Try to keep a grasp of the finances, teach yourself terms you don't know. At some point, of course, you will need professional advice from a lawyer or accountant – and, when you get a manager, you need to delegate and hand over responsibility on many things – but never forget about this side of your career. If you do, it could cost you dearly.

The trick is to recognise when self-management is a double-edged sword. In other words, it's either taking up more time than honing your talent, or you are starting to make mistakes from lack of knowledge or too big a workload. Louis Walsh advises that, for pop hopefuls in particular, self-management is a complete nonstarter. 'For a pop kid it is too much – you can't do it,' he says. 'You can't be honest about yourself. It's essential that you have your bad points pointed out as well as your good ones. Plus, there is just too much to do.'

Depeche Mode were self-managed for much of their career. Andy Franks assisted with their office and saw no adverse effects of this arrangement.

Not having a manager helped them early on, because a seasoned manager would have said, 'Don't go on tour yet again – record another album.' But Daniel [Miller, head of Mute Records] wanted to put records out; he wanted them out on tour because it helped sell the records and the band didn't mind because they loved touring, so it worked.

The Chocolate Speedway Riders were also totally self-managed. OK, our global record sales were not quite as strong as Depeche Mode's (26 copies if you include family and friends, compared with more than 30 million), but we still had to be on the ball. Only once did it really backfire financially, when we played a dingy theme pub/restaurant in Nottingham. We had been promised a fee, almost enough to cover our costs, but after the gig (which admittedly saw several people almost choke on their prawn cocktail) the owner refused to pay up. The problem was, there was no written agreement, so it was his word against ours. We got our own back, though. When he was in the kitchens, we took as many knives and forks as we could fit into our knee-length, luminous shorts. We may have made a two-hundred-mile round trip to play to an audience of two-meals-for-the-price-of-one customers, but we were the only band in London who were never out of cutlery!

PAPA, DON'T PREACH
Many pop artists get their parents to manage them. This can be a good idea at first. Destiny's Child are managed by Beyoncé's father and it certainly hasn't prevented them from becoming one of the biggest acts on the planet. Britney Spears's mother was also heavily involved in her daughter's career. However, remember the old adage that family and business do not always mix. Do you really want to put that sort of strain on your relationship with your parent(s)?

One problem of working with your parents is that they will not be objective. The top songwriters' manager Stephen Budd looks at it like this.

It's so easy for Mum and Dad to say, 'That's wonderful, darling' when their child can string three chords together. When my own six-year-old daughter plays a few notes on the piano I feel the same, but there is a world of difference between parental pride and genuine ability to turn talent into a career. Friends and family aren't objective.

Louis Walsh is equally wary. 'Parents getting involved is OK if they make sure they just help to get a good manager and a good lawyer,' he says, 'but then they need to get out of the way. A lot of showbiz parents bask in the glory of their kids and can be really pushy, but it doesn't work.'

Some managers are often a friend who has learned the business as the artist progresses. This can work brilliantly well, but only if that friend is astute enough. An unknown manager need not necessarily be a stumbling block to getting a record deal. Tony Wadsworth of EMI recalls,

When we signed Coldplay, the manager was like the fifth member of the band. He was a school friend and university mate of theirs. It was obvious he was a really bright guy who was ready to learn and willing to listen. He would always question everything we put forward, which I liked: it's great to be challenged. With more rock-based acts, you sign the act, not the manager, although with pure pop this is less so, obviously.

FINDING A GOOD MANAGER AND AVOIDING THE SHARKS
Selecting a prospective manager is without doubt one of the most important decisions you will make in your entire career. A good one will strongly boost your chances of success; a bad one can leave you penniless with your dreams in tatters. Make sure any prospective manager has *recent* high-profile success with other acts. A one-hit wonder in 1982 with a Scandinavian metal band is not good enough.

Where do you start? You could court your favourite band's manager, but be realistic: people like Louis Walsh are inundated with hundreds of demos a week. EMI's Tony Wadsworth says,

If you are trying to be a pure-pop star, then in reality you do have to prove yourself very, very quickly, otherwise it's 'Next!' The main thing is to have management around you that know the business and have already gone through their learning curve. Make sure you're not going to be one of their big mistakes. There are key people in the pure-pop world who know how to manage these sorts of artists. It isn't any coincidence that Louis Walsh, who manages Westlife, also managed Boyzone and still manages Samantha Mumba.

OK, so you are not going to phone Louis Walsh, get straight through and persuade him to manage you. If you win through on one of his auditions, he will already be there for you. If not, how can you find the right person? Ask around for recommendations – if you've got to the stage where you genuinely need a manager, then you will have numerous contacts of your own: venue owners, sound engineers, other performers. Ask questions. It is a vital decision, so don't make it lightly.

You can at least make the choice an educated one. Albert Samuel, who manages So Solid Crew, offers these tips.

> You should ideally look for a track record, especially in the area of music that you wish to progress in. I do know one or two managers who have started from scratch and been immensely successful – but you wouldn't go to a dentist to work on your entire mouth who'd only been working for two weeks, would you? Other more practical aspects can help too – does he/she have an actual business premises? Check them out with other people. Don't be afraid to ask questions.

A good manager will not be afraid if anyone delves into their business because they will have nothing to hide.

Once you have reassured yourself of a potential manager's credentials, there also has to be a rather more intangible shared belief in your talent. 'The manager's responsibility is to translate what the group's vision is on to a business level,' says Samuel. Without understanding what that vision is, that is impossible.

The premier mixer Dan Frampton is convinced by the power of television and thinks any aspiring new artist – in the pop sphere especially – needs to be aware of this when selecting a manager.

> In the first six months, Steps worked so hard. Fortunately, their management was very well connected in TV. Watching the rise of Steps, I came to the conclusion that TV is what sells modern pop, even more than radio. They appeared on all the early-evening music slots like *Blue Peter* and all the Saturday morning shows too.

So, when you are selecting a manager, think of compatibility. If he has good connections with kids and TV producers but your last song was about the Americanisation of global culture and the evils of the Vietnam War, is he the right man? Conversely, if you aspire to be the next Gareth Gates, then hooking up with a manager who can get you shows at a biker festival might be the worst – and most dangerous – career move you ever make.

Managers should have the same goals and vision for your career. 'They may well stay with you while all around change,' says Stephen Barnes, 'as you go through different record companies, different agents, different PR people. Ask yourself this simple question: if you are not in a meeting, are you confident that your manager will represent your true goals and feelings?'

Once you have found a manager you want to work with and have arranged a meeting to introduce yourself, treat this like any other business meeting. Although in theory you are the client, any prospective manager's first impression of you will affect whether he or she wants to work with you or not. Albert Samuel is often approached by aspiring artists because of his huge success with So Solid Crew. He often sees classic signs of people who have not focused their full attention and ambition on their career, despite thinking otherwise.

If you are really serious about getting into this industry you have to keep in mind it is a severely competitive. Everyone has this ideology that you roll in at 11 a.m. and party all night. My office opens between 9 a.m. and 9.30 a.m. and we're here to do business for our clients. If our clients are still in bed doing nothing, it makes life much more difficult for us. It is a tough, competitive business – a wonderful industry, but you have to accept that sometimes talent alone isn't enough.

Artists sometimes send me an interesting demo and come in to see me. I might mention that their demo wasn't very good quality, so they ask me for money to record a new demo. Yet they will often have come to see me in a four-hundred-pound leather jacket. If you are really serious, how can you go out and spend four hundred pounds on that nice leather jacket when you could have spent that money on your career? How can you expect businesspeople to be committed to your career if you aren't yourself?

So Solid Crew came to Albert through a recommendation from another of his acts, Oxide and Neutrino. The impact of those first few meetings is evident in his recollections.

Megaman came in with a CD and played it to me in my office. Quite frankly, I didn't really get it at the time. It was only listening to it a few times and suddenly understanding it. My view of So Solid was that I never saw it as garage. I always thought they were the new rock 'n' roll. To complement that feeling I had, I was really impressed with the perception of Megaman and G-Man.

They completely got the plot, musically and from a business point of view. They understood it wasn't necessarily about doing the biggest deal straightaway, but more about doing a deal with the right record company. They already immersed everything they did with quality, from photos to videos to demos to shows. There were no quick, easy routes being taken.

How much the manager is involved in the creative process will vary hugely. Pop acts often have much more creatively proactive managers, not least because of the initial balance of power in this genre. 'At first,' explains Louis Walsh, 'you have no hits and no confidence; you do whatever you're manager tells you. As you become more successful and popular, though, you will command a lot more say. Look at Robbie Williams.'

Albert Samuel is more comfortable with less involvement in the creative process. 'Naturally, I might say, "With those lyrics you won't get on Radio 1 or *CD:UK*." But that's about as much as I get involved.'

THE MANAGEMENT CONTRACT
You need to trust your manager, *implicitly*. However, that is not enough. You need a contract, too, to cement your arrangement legally on paper. Sign the wrong thing and you'll be giving a large chunk of the rest of your life away. Don't be naïve – it happens.

The generally accepted fee for a manager is 20 per cent of all income. That means 20 per cent of everything: recording, publishing, touring, merchandise and so on. Remember, too, that this is 20 per cent of the gross figure. Simply put, if you get £100 for a show and it costs you £40 to get there, your manager will earn 20 per cent of £100, namely £20. So you receive £100 for the show, you pay the travel costs of £40 and the management fee of £20, leaving you with £40. Only double the amount your manager has received!

At this initial agreement stage, you must be absolutely crystal clear what your manager is taking 20 per cent of. All management contracts differ – some take 20 per cent of the total amount you are paid before expenses and costs; many others take 20 per cent of the amounts received *after* costs, which is obviously preferable to the artist.

Former All Saint Natalie Appleton's advice is, 'Don't sign anything. Get a manager by all means but just see how it develops for a while. If you think things are going well and you trust them, then by all means commit to signing something, but not before you've built up trust.'

If you do sign a management contract very early on, try to keep it to just three months. From the very beginning, set ground rules about expenses. If a manager says, 'I'm coming over to your show in Paris' it is at their expense. But if you say, 'Come on over' you should be paying for it. Avoid confusion that can create great animosity and friction.

PROBLEMS TO LOOK OUT FOR

Don't be lazy. Just because you have a manager, don't suddenly forget about every element of your career except the performance. A successful artist is an entire package and, if you want your career to go to plan, you need to know what is going on.

You also need to remain aware of the manager's contribution to your career. Good managers will make things happen that you can't; bad managers will just process developments that come to you through your own work or unsolicited. Paying them 20 per cent for just doing that is futile and expensive.

Another common problem is that many managers take 20 per cent from a pop star but want to live a 100-per-cent rock-and-roll lifestyle. Many acts run into severe problems because of this. When any money is paid to an artist or act, I recommend strongly that it should go straight into the artist's bank account. The artist then pays whoever they owe money too. The record business is littered with tales of scams, so be careful. It is not unheard of for an artist to have the advance for a record deal paid to their manager and that's the last time they saw either the manager or the money.

Your manager should not also be your accountant or your lawyer. The manager should run the business, but the financial aspects of that business need to be in the hands of an expert. Some of the best managers have got either a legal or accounting background, but they should not be the same person.

By contrast, Albert Samuel believes that many of the fabled manager–artist rip-offs are becoming increasingly uncommon.

It is getting less and less prevalent as the business becomes more and more structured. These days, music-industry lawyers will happily advise an artist not to sign any contract if it simply isn't feasible. So appoint a good music-industry lawyer and not one that happens to be the brother of a sister of a friend.

Finally, if you are trying to audition to become a pure-pop act, then the management may well come to you. Chances are that the future manager of the band will be in the panel of judges you are performing before. Similarly, if you truly are a genuine undiscovered talent, the managers will come to you.

So you might well ask if you need to worry about this chapter. You do. Exactly the same rules apply for vetting prospective management.

9. ALL ABOUT AGENTS

'Some of those club owners were crazy. There was one guy pulled out a gun one night and shot an amplifier . . . smoke curling up to the ceiling. Absolute quiet. And he says, "I told you to turn it down."' Bruce Springsteen, discussing his early live shows

The role of a pop star's agent is essentially to book shows. That could be a slot at a local variety club or a three-night stint at Wembley Arena. Just as with a manager, whether you want to be the new Darius or the next Green Day, you do not need an agent. An agent is not someone to employ to boost your ego. Those endless early shows that you play will be valuable learning tools for you to arrange your own shows and find out how live work pays. Advice about getting early live experience is contained in Chapter 4. If you aren't suitably motivated enough to book your own shows when you start, put this book down and go and do a different job.

As we saw briefly in that chapter, one of the problems you will be facing is the lack of performance opportunities, again both for solo stars and acts. Twenty years ago Britain was still alive with chances for singers and groups to learn their trade and get regular work: working men's clubs, social clubs, British Legion clubs, cruise ships, hotels, holiday camps . . . They were the places where young performers would learn their craft and get the all-too-valuable experience on stage. In 'the good old days' there were endless opportunities – TV stars topped the bill, and down the list would be dozens of lesser-known acts all looking for a big break. An act could work a different club every night for six months without travelling more than a few dozen miles from home, and at the end of the six months could start the circuit again, so filling the whole year-long diary with engagements without too much difficulty.

These days it's a different story. With fewer clubs, there are fewer opportunities and the big stars demand such high fees that many venues can no longer afford to take lesser acts on board too (not for a fee, anyway). This often means that new and unheard-of performers find themselves much nearer the top of the bill in smaller venues than in the old days, because the stars themselves won't play and there are fewer artists in a given night's line-up. So promoters and agents are looking for quality acts who can deliver the goods regularly. With so many college and university courses spilling out trained singers and great sight-reading musicians, there is a lot of competition for the jobs available – another reason, perhaps, for you to consider formal training of some sort (see Chapter 14).

Sadly, this circuit has all but disappeared in recent years, although there are still frequent opportunities for live work at social functions, weddings and so on, if you are keen enough. Such gigs can be a vital place for your career to start, and you need to approach this part of the market with the same professionalism and realism as you would an audition to be the next Will Young.

Despite these challenges, if your hard work is starting to pay off and you are getting more enquiries and interest, you might start to worry that your inexperience or sheer workload is causing your live potential to underachieve. Accessing this shrinking market will be easier with an agent, but how on earth do you go about getting one? There are two levels of agents, both of which apply to differing degrees for solo performers and acts.

1. AGENTS AT A LOCAL LEVEL
As we've seen, the local scene really is the place in which so much groundwork will be done for your later years at the top of the charts. Getting a good agent at the right time can help to maximise your impact at a local level and sharpen your potential.

Ideally, a personal recommendation is the best way to source an agent. Maybe you could go to a club where a known local singer or act is performing – with a guardian if you are underage – and politely ask them for their own agent's details or, if they are reluctant (you're potential competition), ask for alternatives. Venue owners will always be a great source of contacts, too. It is in their interests to find new talent to keep their own business vibrant. Failing that, industry reference books such as *Music Week Directory* or more public sources such as the *Yellow Pages* will list entertainment agencies or companies who book acts and place them in work locally, nationally and often overseas. These companies are often the best starting point for you or your band, but be very wary and cynical. It is an age-old tip never to trust people who have pictures of themselves on the wall with famous people. This might be a little over-cautious, but don't be fooled by glitz – this is a business decision.

Once you have highlighted an agent you want to work with,

approaching that prospective colleague needs to be done in a calculated and professional manner. Have your CD and photo ready, not 'about to be recorded'. They haven't got time for this. Explain your goals and ideas about where you want to go. Once they've listened to the demo, ask for their objective opinion, query where they think you can go. If they say, 'Sorry, love, you'll be lucky to break on to the pie-and-mash circuit, never mind *Pop Idol*,' don't be patronised or offended – it is only one opinion. Conversely, if their office is a flat above a chip shop and their biggest act is an Elvis tribute, be wary if they say, 'You're the best voice I've heard since the King – I'll make you millions.' Apart from the fact they're possibly stretching the truth, by saying, 'I'll make you millions', they mean, '*You'll* make *me* millions.' Better to find that you are working towards totally opposite goals now than later, when you are waiting for a booking for Wembley Arena and instead you get Wembley Pensioners' Club.

Don't forget, too, that, like good managers, agents make a living from their talent, so they will be out there looking for you. They won't find you if you are sitting at home watching *Star For a Night* mumbling about how much better you are than any of 'them idiots' on the telly, so this is where your early live experience will generate local profile. Persevere – eventually you'll find a good agent who just might be the missing piece in your jigsaw puzzle.

Sylvia Young has this advice to offer about finding a local agent.

> Send a good black-and-white head shot with some details about yourself to them. When you are brought in for an interview, don't be afraid to ask questions, but be cautious: a good agent won't take kindly to being queried on their reputation. The ones to ask more probing questions of are the ones that advertise in papers. They can be less reputable – although, having said that, when I first started a long time ago, I advertised in a local paper, so you have got to start somewhere!

As general advice, if a fee is going to be charged for 'registering' you with an agent, it should be stated in the advert. Auditions should always be free and you should be told what they are for. You shouldn't pay any money at all in advance and don't meet agents alone at private addresses.

Many agents are former or currently working professionals themselves, and many will have been in the business since before you were born. You won't fool anyone. If you're no good, they won't take you on, because they'll very quickly get a reputation for booking and placing poor acts and begin to lose business themselves. If they do like you, they will get you work on the local pub-and-club circuit, playing in dodgy places where you might want to wipe your feet on the way *out*. Remember, though, that any live work is brilliant experience and, if you are getting paid for that, even a few pounds, you are doing very well.

Once you get an agent, fame will not necessarily follow overnight. It could be months, more likely years. If you work well in the small venues and give the punters what they want night after night, without complaining and without causing your agent too many headaches, you may get booked for bigger shows and higher-profile events. Many agencies now concentrate on corporate events and weddings – big companies look for entertainment at their major sales conferences – and a good singer or band can work regularly in these venues while they learn their craft.

Cruise ships, ferryboats and holiday camps used to be great venues for regular work, but, as holiday habits change and more people travel abroad, these opportunities are fewer. They still exist and are a great vehicle for entertainers of all disciplines. Historically, many agents have booked their acts abroad in major such as like Dubai and Bahrain, but, again, the competition in these places has grown fiercely over the years and bands from all over the world compete for ever-decreasing fees. If you can get foreign work, though, it will do you good in the long run, as you learn more about different kinds of venues and audiences.

It is vital, however, not to let your enthusiasm for working these local circuits blur your focus and vision. If you want what can be a solid career as a club singer, then you need to graft just as hard and probably need a thicker skin than even a pop idol. However, if your sights are truly set on the kind of fame enjoyed by a select few, *keep your eyes on the prize*.

In the interests of accuracy, it is important that I point out that some of the most successful performers sing in clubs every night. Top club and cruise singers can earn very serious amounts of money. Some of the happiest people play pubs, yet some of the unhappiest people in the business are playing the main stage at Glastonbury. A lot of club singers end up with far more than artists who sign these fabled million-pound deals. And you don't need to be Jane McDonald to make a very good living from club work. I'm guessing, because you have bought or borrowed this book, that club singing is not your aim, but don't dismiss it out of hand.

One final tip with local agents. Once you've signed your major-label deal and everyone wants to book you and talk to you, *never* forget your roots. If you make it on to *Top of the Pops* and earn a million pounds in six months, never forget the local agent who got you started. Always treat them with respect even if you move up to a major record company and a top-line agency. Hard to imagine, perhaps, but one day your star may fade and you may well need these guys again on the way down, or while you rebuild your failing career. It's a natural progression from obscurity to fame and back again, and the people who helped you in the beginning can keep your flame alive in later years. Or extinguish it altogether.

2. AGENTS AT A NATIONAL LEVEL

This is more likely to involve you if you are pursuing a high-profile career rather than a steady club lifestyle. The same rules still apply to getting a good agent: ask for recommendations, look at other acts on their roster and don't be afraid to ask questions. However, the likelihood is that if your talent is beginning to get noticed to the extent that you need an agent, the good ones will probably come looking for you. As with A & R people, word of mouth within agents' circles is the fuel for their fire and you may find you get approached by several reputable agents all at once. Let's hope so.

As we saw earlier, Nigel Hassler is one of the music business's top agents, boasting scores of superstars on his roster at Helter Skelter. His advice about agents is priceless.

As you are aware, the core role of an agent is to book shows. The vast majority do that on a commission-only basis – usually 15 per cent. However, it is more proactive than that simple statement suggests. A good agent will be able to nurture an artist's live career, and strategise the positioning of an act's or performer's development through careful selection of venues, using the right promoters, support tours and so on. The right agent can take you from almost no fan base to arena tours on a global basis.

As with my word of caution about local agents, Nigel also advises that, even with a nationally reputable agent on board, don't expect fame or riches to be just around the corner.

When you've signed your first record deal and are playing to three hundred people a night, you'll be lucky to be covering your costs. It's purely a promotional exercise at that stage. Even when you get to much bigger venues, playing to, say, two thousand people a night, your friends will all say you're making a fortune, but the problem is that the stakes are much higher. Whereas at your earlier shows your dad drove the van and your mate humped gear, now you've got to pay for articulate drivers, roadies, guitar techs and so on.

As for the initial meeting with the big-name agent, Nigel has this to say:

If you're approached by an agent for a meeting, you shouldn't be nervous because at that stage it means they've heard your music or talent and like it. The agent will only ask for that meeting if there is a serious chance of your working with them. As far as how you carry yourself in the meeting [is concerned], certainly for my type of acts, it is almost irrespective of how you look really, especially if you are young. We are aware people can be developed and polished. I've never been interested in a new band and then met them only to be put off.

When Oasis were signed [by Nigel's previous agency, Primary Talent], they used to shamble on stage, all scruffy, but there was such an attitude, you had to be aware of the long-term potential. Musically they were OK, but Liam was just great. They were playing to three hundred people and had had very little press. They were only getting fifty pounds at the time, so a colleague of mine, Ben Winchester, signed them at Primary Talent.

Nigel has seen this artist development work with one of his big acts, the Lighthouse Family. Their transformation into one of the country's biggest live propositions is exactly the sort of example of an agent–artist relationship that you should be looking for. Nigel says,

I signed the Lighthouse Family when they hadn't had any record releases. I was sent a five-track sampler of their forthcoming album and I just thought the songs were magnificent. I was thinking along the lines of Simply Red and huge potential. The problem was there was no organic fan base, so at that stage they could have either broken huge or done nothing at all. We met them, signed them and started our plan.

They had no touring history whatsoever, even though their album sampler was highly polished. The challenge was to build their life profile sufficiently to catch up with the standard of their records and radio profile. Initially, they were terrible live. There was no stage presence, no charisma, and we had to work very hard to build their confidence and tweak the band. I first saw them play at the Canal Bar in Manchester to eight people. With us on board, progression was made and they were playing to three hundred people in London, but the problem was that two hundred of those attending were from the record business – no ordinary punters to speak of. Then slowly they started to get more confidence, the singer came out of his shell and they became a great live band.

Six years after that first Manchester show, they played four nights at Wembley Arena to forty thousand people. What I had seen as long-term potential had manifested itself. Whether you are pop or rock the goals are the same: building a live profile, generating that fan base. Pop might use more TV and radio and less live touring, but the goals are essentially the same.

I know what you are thinking. Why don't I just phone Nigel or another national agent and leapfrog from the local pub to Brixton Academy? If only it were that simple! First, you will not be good enough. Second, agencies are businesses, not charities.

At the level where you are working locally [Nigel continues], having a major agent calling a venue to book a gig doesn't really make any difference. We can't make money from an act being paid a hundred pounds a night.

You will more than likely already have a manager on board by the time you need a major agent, so his role in the selection process will be key, too. More often than not, this will be after a record deal, because a top agent aims to work in tandem with a product that can be promoted, namely a single or album.

By the way, in case you were wondering, the nearest the Chocolate Speedway Riders ever got to someone like Nigel Hassler was a travel agent. There was never much call for a band with no following, no talent, no future and no money. People in the music business can be so fussy . . .

10. 'MANUFACTURED' POP

'The best bands are tribes.' Henry Rollins

Everything we've looked at so far is vital to your chances of becoming a pop star. Even if you are one of the chosen few who are selected to be part of a so-called 'manufactured pop' act, then all of the above is still essential. Indeed, you will probably have had to go through all of these stages to get to the stage of being selected at all. That said, there are some elements of being in such a manufactured band that are unique and need some explanation here.

Just as *Pop Idol* makes the public the talent scout, artist managers such as Simon Fuller work together with production houses, first to audition and then to package bands that arrive at the record-company meeting perfectly polished and ready for the charts. It is a monumental skill and such managers are multitalented experts. If you have one of these people on your side, you are in pole position.

How do you get to that point, though? We've already looked at auditions and this is the core of how these bands are discovered. Auditions are the obvious starting point, but not the only one. Hugh Goldsmith of Innocent Records believes pop hopefuls can learn from the story of Blue and perhaps take more from a rock band's more organic development.

> Myself and Daniel Glatman, Blue's manager, went out there looking for new talent, searching high and low, through the obvious ads in the *Stage* but also through all our networks on the ground. Who is out there? Who have we seen? Who has he seen? Who have I seen? Who are we aware of? Through that process, we met a couple of the guys from Blue who we really liked but, after that start, the rest of the act put themselves together. They had friends they wanted us to meet, who we then auditioned after being introduced. They still had to prove themselves to us. We put them through their paces. So Blue coming together was much more organic.
>
> I am encouraging aspiring pop stars more and more to build it up themselves at first, then later with my assistance in the

background. That way, when you are on the road and you've been together every waking moment for a year and a half, you are less likely to see a band split.

Hugh thinks that the more natural process of Blue's coming together has helped them receive more credibility in the marketplace, something you should perhaps consider when you are working your own way into a new band. 'Blue have a lot of respect in the marketplace,' says Hugh. 'They get a lot of good press from cutting-edge publications, they get played by cutting-edge radio stations and they have the respect of the media. They're genuinely brilliant singers and they genuinely have a camaraderie between them. Significant talent is critical.'

Another example of the unconventional surfacing of a pop star is that of Billie Piper. 'I saw her in a TV ad for *Smash Hits* magazine,' recounts Hugh, 'and I thought, "She's a star." I had no idea if she could sing, but I tracked her down to Sylvia Young's Stage School.'

Atomic Kitten came to Hugh Goldsmith through a management contact, Martin O'Shea. Hugh continues the story.

They are all from the Liverpool area and Martin and Andy McCluskey had already formed the band. I went to see them at a showcase and after they finished the first song I told him that they had got a record deal. I didn't need to see more than a minute of the band to know that they were definitely something I was looking for. They were the antithesis of everything that was going on in the market at the time. They were earthy, real and in your face and they had some great pop songs, too – it just felt right.

Hugh's belief that pop acts should be prepared to hone their talent and form bands themselves to begin with is shared by Louis Walsh.

Any pop act needs to get on well, otherwise forget about it. Try to get some friends together, even go so far as auditioning together. This is what Westlife were doing. There were six of them from Sligo playing in a band called IOU, but only three made it into Westlife. I saw that original six in IOU and got them on supporting the Backstreet Boys. I thought only three of them were good, Kian, Mark and Shane, so we had to weed out the other three. We had auditions in Dublin attended by a few hundred people and that's where we got Nicky and Brian from.

Richard Smith works with many pop acts and often uses another non-audition strategy. He agents live shows for Blazin' Squad, who are an acutely successful example of a meticulously planned strategy that always develops this style of young act. Richard is renowned for his knowledge of what is called the 'PA' circuit. A PA is where a performer or act sings to a backing DAT (digital audio tape) rather than totally live. It is through relentless PAs that Blazin' Squad have generated enough groundswell of support to get to number one with their debut single 'Crossroads'. If you intend to be in a pop act, you have to face the fact that at some point it is highly likely that you will have to follow this route. Even if you win through the auditions and are selected for the band, you still have a gruelling workload ahead of you.

Sometimes [says Richard] an act will do what we call a 'top and tail', whereby they say 'hello' at the start and then 'thank you' at the end of the show. People say this is a cop-out but the simple reason we do that sometimes is that at a majority of nightclubs the PA systems are notoriously poor quality. Many of these aspiring pop stars will be doing a 'double', namely two shows in one night at two different clubs, so there won't even be time for any kind of sound check.

The snipers are quick to criticise acts like Blazin' Squad unfairly as lightweight pop without the years of touring behind them, but again this is no easy option, according to Richard.

Leading up to the release of an act's first single, they will do club PAs, TV appearances and probably in the region of twenty-five major radio PAs like 'Party in the Park', so all in all about fifty gigs. It's a question of getting in front of the most possible people in that important period. Think about this if you are booking your own shows – if you do a gig two months ahead of a release, that club are going to have another PA the next week and the next and the next, so by the time your record is released those punters have forgotten about you.

But how do we get a PA without a top manager like Blazin' Squad's Albert Samuel? I hear you cry. Richard Smith says,

It's a question of sending them a package and then picking up the phone and ringing the venue. Be enthusiastic and say, 'Hi, here we are, this is what we look like, here is a copy of our CD, this is what we sound like.' If you are good at selling yourself and you get a PA, you will be lucky to get fifty pounds expenses. Blazin' Squad got that or nothing. Free shows are part and parcel of the promotion. So, if you drive somewhere long-distance, you will probably have spent more on petrol by the time you arrive at the venue than you will earn for your night's work.

One of the circuits you will be working is schools. The reason pop acts target schools and younger clubs is very simple: the vast majority of the singles-buying market is under sixteen. Richard says that schools tours have become very popular now, whereas, years ago, they didn't really exist.

Bros were one of the very first acts to do school tours. It was a very new concept back then. Now there are specific companies that do schools tours. You turn up at a school assembly at nine in the morning and do a PA as part of the morning assembly. It is a captive audience and a perfect demograph. You do a load of schools in the morning, club PAs in the evening and get to as many possible people in a single day. The only thing to bear in mind is that a school PA is virtually impossible without an agent or manager, simply because you have to provide your own PA system, which will be just too expensive for an unsigned act.

Richard has another word of warning for any pop acts thinking they can go the manufactured/PA route without any assistance.

The mistake many pop acts make is that they assume that performing hundreds of PAs will automatically do the trick. However, the key point is that you have to have so many other elements in place to work in conjunction with those PAs. I know lots of aspiring pop stars who get out there and work hard, doing shows at schools and clubs and especially on the under-eighteen circuit, but they have no infrastructure in place.

For example, they are going in there, getting these kids to fill in forms, but not even selling a product. Kids will fill in any form! If it's free, they'll fill it in! It will get them on the mailing list but unless you feed that interest that 'fan' will very quickly jump to the next available band. A prospective record company will not sign you because you have five hundred names on a mailing list – if they want a database, they just buy one. I could probably name twenty acts out there that are touring around doing this, and it's not going to work.

Even if you triumph and get selected for a manufactured band, you need to be aware whether or not the chemistry within the group is working. That's not to say because you don't like 'the pretty one' you should throw what might be your only shot at fame in the trash. Just be aware of the importance of personality for any band – just because you win an audition and get a part, just because the manager is a known heavyweight and the record companies are circling like vultures, the people within the band are still the ones whose interpersonal magic could make or break their chances. You still have work to do!

'I don't think people always gave the Spice Girls credit for what they achieved,' muses Tony Wadsworth of EMI. He continues,

I admit they were brilliantly managed by Simon Fuller, but also one of the reasons why they were so massively successful was that within that group of five people there was a lot of drive and determination, a lot of ideas, wit and energy. It wasn't just slung together, even though they originally came together from an advert. After that initial creation, they developed something special within themselves and I believe that is what people related to on such a huge scale.

Richard Smith has some harsh facts for similar female hopefuls.

In my opinion, in the pop world it is harder to break a female act than a male act. Simply put, little girls are more passionate than young men. At a girl's concert, you don't have rows and rows of teenage boys at the front screaming up at the stage. This affects even those who succeed. Kylie's audience is predominantly girls and gay men. All men seem to fancy Kylie, she is beautiful, but I wouldn't stand at a concert and scream at her.

Look at *Pop Idol*. A girl was never going to win that. Look at the charts, there have been a lot more big boy bands over the years than girl bands. There was the Spice Girls of course, and more recently we have Atomic Kitten and before that B*Witched. It's not unheard of, but the boys' list is, by comparison, endless.

Another popular misconception about manufactured pop acts is that the workload will be any lighter. Big mistake. Cordelia Plunkett has worked with S Club 7.

They are known as one of the hardest-working acts in the business. They do sixteen-, seventeen-hour days all the time and are telling me that was an easy day! It is hard to get hold of them some days because they are always working. You see them grabbing quick cat naps on the road or between takes just to try to refuel. They are the hardest working band I've been involved in, putting in quite horrific hours. Their work ethic is frightening, they are so dedicated.

Louis Walsh is not afraid to say that pop acts have the more severe workload. 'Pop acts have to work twice as hard as rock acts, definitely,' he says, and continues,

They have to because it's all about selling yourself to the kids. They have to do more TV shows, more gigs more signings – everything. Oasis and Coldplay are great, great bands but they don't have to work as hard – they have Radio 1, *Q* magazine and *NME* for example, but we never get that. We have to work harder for our slots. Plus, there is so much more pressure on a pop act. Their career is shorter and the failure rate is so much higher. Record companies pay for choreographers, stylists, security, producers, expensive videos, photo shoots, tour mangers – it's all money. Money they will want to earn back.

Furthermore, you have to appreciate that the financial pressures on a pure-pop band are far greater than a rock act. Echo Records' David Rowell says,

With pure pop, the money being spent is still not any guarantee. I've seen artists spend five hundred thousand pounds on a promo campaign, record complete albums, employ the best pluggers and PR people, then sell about five hundred copies of a single, after which they've sunk without trace. If you include a video, tour buy-ons and other costs, the figures are frightening. Even if you succeed, you might need to sell five hundred thousand albums to make financial sense of your project.

When such vast sums are being spent on these pop acts, sceptical critics are bound to be numerous and vocal. One of the frequent accusations fired at manufactured pop acts is that they cannot sing. Richard Smith suggests that, just as with rock acts who are aiming for the Mercury Music Prize, within the context of the pop market, any hopefuls have to sound good.

The record has to stand up on its own. It doesn't matter how good you are on stage if the record is no good. A lot of the unsigned bands in this genre are flying around spending so much time choreographing themselves and getting good stage outfits, but the quality of the recording is awful. They'd be better off spending some time and money having vocal lessons for example.

Likewise, dance is becoming increasingly important in pop. Many top sportsmen and sportswomen have benefited from ballet and dance classes: they improve your movement on stage in lots of different ways. Even if your act won't require you to dance, it is worth it; and, if you're a solo singer whose movement on stage *will* be scrutinised, then dance classes are essential. Clearly, if you play thrash music that kills pigeons at fifty paces, you won't be needing the leg warmers and a leotard – but think about whether there is any lateral advantage to your having some basic knowledge.

Cordelia Plunkett suggests you can work around any disadvantages.

For the pop angle, good dancing ability, photogenic looks and so on are a given. You will be groomed of course, but there has to be some degree of these basic prerequisites to get chosen in the first place. If you look good but have two left feet, that might cause problems for a pop wannabe. However, not everyone can afford dancing lessons, so you need to do what you can. Watch pop videos, mimic the moves, learn at home. Get your mates round and make it a good night, relax and have a go at it. Over time, you will pick the moves up so that in the next audition you are arming yourself with as many advantages as you can.

By contrast, Westlife's manager Louis Walsh is not always looking for a new Fred Astaire, because dancing isn't always vital. 'It wasn't to Westlife or to Blue,' he says. 'If you're trying to be a great vocal act, dancing is not necessary. That said, Take That were one of the best boy bands I've ever seen at putting on a live show: they always did such brilliant dancing. N'Sync look dreadful but they are great dancers.'

ISSUES WITH AGE

Before you put this book down and say, 'I don't need to worry, I'm only young,' think again. Music has traditionally been the domain of the young, particularly in the pop genre. There is a long history of chart acts breaking through in their teens or even before that. Michael Jackson first sang live when he was just four, and signed a solo deal at fourteen. Little Jimmy Osmond was on top of the charts with 'Long-Haired Lover from Liverpool' aged just eight. I thought S Club 7 looked remarkably young until I saw S Club Juniors, who were positively infant. Britney Spears's debut single was a global smash when she was just fifteen.

If you aspire to be a pop star, that is your level of competition. Look at the video for 'Hit Me Baby . . .' Britney looks fantastic. The award-winning dance routines are superb. Britney herself dances seamlessly alongside seasoned (albeit young) professional dancers. Listen to her vocal, the small nuances she puts down on some line endings or between lyrics without ever actually overdoing the effect. Then view the overall package again. It is flawless pop. That is why it was number one. That is why Britney went past that initial hit to become one of the modern era's most successful solo pop stars. Then remember this: she started working on this first record project when she was just fourteen. She was singing professionally from the age of eight. So no more excuses about your age.

Indeed, use your age to your advantage. You have to understand that experience is something you earn, not something you can buy, but at the same time don't be intimidated. You are bulletproof, your naïveté and energy provide a head start over the older more experienced hopefuls. 'The younger ones are far more resilient!' muses Sylvia Young. 'You also find that many children don't have the same fears as adults when it comes to appearing on the stage, they are just looking forward to it so much.'

Korda Marshal of Mushroom Records loves working with young stars.

The first time I saw Matt Bellamy from Muse he was only seventeen. He was clearly a genius musician even then. One minute he was playing classic Jimi Hendrix riffs on his guitar, then he would sit down and play Rachmaninov or Bach. Many of the really talented artists are found by the record industry at a very early age. Kate Bush was signed at fifteen. That degree of talent is so rare.

One thing you should consider is what the practical repercussions may be if you go for an audition while still at school – and succeed. It is easy to say you will fit things in but the reality is not that simple. You might give up school, or work so little that your final grades are under par, relying on the notion that your pop career will see you right. Bad idea. For one thing, pop careers can be notoriously brief; for another, the money may not always be as good as you thought (see Chapter 11). You could find yourself at twenty – as many failed or fleeting pop stars have – on the pop scrap heap with no money, no job and no qualifications.

On a practical level, Sylvia Young explains how young performers in some genres 'have to be licensed to perform, which means you send a form in to the education authority, have a health check and an agreement from the school giving permission to miss classes. There are less restrictions now than there used to be, but you must still do things properly.'

Hugh Goldsmith of Innocent Records tells how he signed Billie Piper when she was very young.

I thought Billie was older than she actually was. As a general rule I wouldn't and won't sign artists who are under sixteen. I think people need to have some teenage years, grow up a bit, have a normal life. It makes them more mature and you don't then have this horrible feeling as a record executive that you have just taken the key formative years out of an individual's life.

In the rock sphere it is less common but still not impossible to see very young acts break through. Korda Marshall signed the Northern Ireland band Ash when the lead singer and chief songwriter, Tim, was just fifteen. Korda picks up the story:

I was out for a drink with a noted music press officer and his girlfriend. She was being very derisory about the London music scene, saying we were too myopic. Then she said, 'The best band in the world comes from my little village called Downpatrick in Northern Ireland. They're better than all your new demos and all your new bands.' We went over to Downpatrick and stayed at Tim's house, drinking brandy late into the night with his dad, then we were up having breakfast with his mom first thing in the morning after she had walked the dogs. Ash all went off to school and then we saw them perform that day at the local arts centre. There was a play first, followed by numerous local bands doing twenty-minute sets, one of which was Ash. The audience was aged only seven to about thirteen. Tim was fantastic and Ash immediately reminded me so much of Nirvana.

Ash had a garage where the band could rehearse. Tim's parents had helped him by buying a guitar. His brother had a great record collection, which Tim was astute enough to listen to and be influenced by. In their school holidays they went on tour with Elastica and then did some of their own dates, but even at that young age there was a very strong work ethic. Like anything in life, you get out of it what you put in.

Despite what I saw as great musical quality, it was made very clear that, until they had finished their exams, school was the priority. I had to guarantee to their school headmaster that I wouldn't put a record into the top forty prior to their doing their A levels, because he didn't want them on *Top of the Pops* distracting them from their studies. That's the first time in my career I've had to write a letter to a headmaster! So we scheduled in the single 'Girl From Mars', which came out the day they got their A-level results and subsequently went top forty.

11. CONTRACTS AND LEGAL ISSUES

'As an adult I have been willing to say, "OK, I'm gonna do the business" because out of that business I get to do the art, I get to do the music.'
Melissa Etheridge

Turn your stereo off, sit down in a room on your own and read this chapter. It could turn out to be among the most important few minutes of your entire career.

You are trying to enter the business of making music. In any business, people make products or offer services, which they sell. The quicker you get used to the fact that you are a commodity and you make and sell a product, the better. You may not like it and it may even offend your artistic sensibilities, but it is a fact. Your record company will hopefully share your vision and understand your creative foibles and goals, but chances are that if you sell fewer records than an Elvis impersonator their interest in your 'business' will end.

If you have been working hard at all the areas covered by this book and have genuine talent, there may come a time when someone decides they want to work with you. To those of you who have a record deal on the table, I have two comments to make.

- One: Bloody well done. You are among a tiny elite of performers who ever get approached with such a proposition. You must have worked painfully hard to get to that point.
- Two: This could be the most precarious position you will ever be in. Indeed, you could be about to throw it all away: your career, your financial future and your chance at stardom. This is very serious indeed.

In this chapter, we will look at the two key elements that you need to know about with regard to contracts: the financial repercussions and the legal implications. This is meant only as a summary of the almost infinite permutations and complications you might encounter, merely to educate you on the basics. Before going any further, if you have got to this point, you *must* get a music-business lawyer and a specialist accountant.

MONEY AND MUSIC

Dave Clark owns DPC Media, an accountancy firm who look after numerous music-business clients, among them the Prodigy. This Essex band have sold in excess of 30 million records worldwide in dozens of countries and in 1997 became only the seventh British band ever to enter the American album charts straight at number one with their third album *The Fat of the Land*. The financial implications of such a massive career are manifold and you do not need to know every detail here. However, Dave is disarmingly blunt about the financial quagmire that many artists – and indeed aspiring artists – get themselves into.

So read this chapter carefully. Don't skip it because it's about 'boring stuff'. If you do, then you have only yourself to blame when you've sold three gold albums, you're skint and your record company tells you that you still owe them £500,000.

You are trying to get noticed and at this stage all you want is for someone to offer you a record deal. Yet, that is only one aspect of the business. In simple terms you are looking for:

- a record contract
- a publishing contract
- other income sources

A RECORD CONTRACT

A record contract is usually but not always the first contract you will sign. It is an agreement – usually exclusive – between yourself (or yourselves if you're a band) and a record label that wishes to exploit your material or talent commercially. This will cover every form: CD, video, vinyl, cassette, DVD, Mini Disc, CD-ROM and so on.

You will agree an advance for your record contract. If you've done well, that might be £250,000. You get this news from your manager and nearly break the polystyrene covering on your parents' ceiling jumping for joy. Next step? Sit down and listen.

A portion will be payable on signing the contract – let's say £100,000. You are then expected to go away and produce your album or material. You will get another portion – let's say £75,000 – on delivery of the album. The record company are then allowed to decide whether or not what you have delivered to them is complete rubbish. If they accept the material, the final part of your advance is generally on the release of the record, which is often within a few months of the delivery. Furthermore, advances are generally recoupable but not refundable, so if your contract is terminated (if, in other words, you are released by the label) you will keep the money. So, feasibly, if you sign the deal and deliver an acceptable album that is then released within twelve months, you will receive a figure of £250,000. Not bad for a year's work, eh? Change those flights to first class and start getting your groceries delivered for you – from Harrods.

Er, no. Now the bad news.

There are many costs and expenses that you need to be aware of, as Dave Clark explains.

First, you will have to pay the lawyers who worked on your record contract for you. These people are specialists and therefore not cheap. Expect to pay anywhere between five thousand and fifty thousand pounds, depending on the length of contract and size of deal. Secondly, if you've been sensible, you will have paid an accountant to overlook the financial clauses. That could be another five thousand pounds.

Then you have a manager to pay. Working on a standard fee of twenty per cent, we'll use the admittedly more onerous arrangement, although a not uncommon one, that he is entitled to that percentage of the headline figure, namely two hundred and fifty thousand pounds. Then you will have a tax bill on these earnings, which, presuming you haven't paid for good accountancy advice, you will be paying at the top rate of forty per cent.

So, breaking this down into simple terms we have:

Entire record advance: £250,000
Legal costs: £20,000
Accountancy costs: £5,000
Manager's fee: £50,000 (20% of £250,000)
Tax (approximate): £70,000
Subtotal remaining: £105,000

That's OK, I hear you say – I can cope with £105,000 being put into my bank account. Think again. This money might have to last you for two or three years. If your record fails to set the charts alight and you end up with no record deal and your stardom is over, that amount is not going to enable you to retire. You might end up with an aggregate of £35,000 a year for three years possibly, yet your friends read the headline about £250,000, so it's always your round at the local. This works if you are a solo artist. You don't need to be Stephen Hawking to realise that if there are seven of you in the band, because you absolutely *had* to have that extra glockenspiel to fulfil your complete artistic statement, your £35,000 is suddenly a lot less. Possibly as low as £12,000 in total. For three years' living costs!

You forgot about your album, too. You need to record that and it needs to be done in a quality studio. That might cost an awful lot of money. A top studio could cost you £700 a day with engineers and all other necessary personnel. If you manage to record the album for £50,000, you have to pay for some of that yourself (if that sounds a lot, consider that most top chart acts spend on average £20,000 on studio costs for a single). Don't worry: the record company will pay half of the bill, but the remaining £25,000 is your share, which will be added to your debt/advance, which is already at £250,000. That debt is growing and you haven't released a single note yet. So don't sit at the back of a studio, chatting with your mates on your mobile telling them how exciting it is – it will be the most expensive mobile-phone call you ever make. As with demo work, if budgets are tight, try to write and work on your material before you enter the studio. Again, this may be advice for after a record deal, but one day you will have your first session in a studio, so you need to know.

That's OK, you say, my records are going to sell so many copies that I will recoup this advance (namely pay it back) and then start earning royalties on top in no time. That pink Porsche 911 I've had custom-sprayed will be on my drive in three weeks and it will all be paid for soon. Wrong.

Let's say you do well. Very well. Your debut single gets to number one. You go on *Top of the Pops*. Even your uncle now sees that you're a pop star. You'll be loaded, right? Wrong again.

If we just look at the income solely from your number-one single, it could break down as follows. The record company pays you a royalty on every single sold. To get to the top of the charts you might need to sell only 25,000 singles, depending on who else is releasing that week (for your sake, hopefully not anyone from *Pop Idol* or *Popstars*). So you might typically get paid 15 per cent of what is called the 'PPD' or 'dealer price'. This is a figure set by the record company and for a single might be around £2. However, the record company is entitled to deduct packaging costs, which might be as high as 25 per cent. So here's the breakdown:

Singles cost in the shop: £3.99
PPD or dealer price – say £2.00
Packaging costs: 25% of £2.00 = £0.50
Subtotal: £2.00 – £0.50 = £1.50
Your royalty: 15% of £1.50, namely 22.5p
Singles sold to get to number one in the charts: 25,000
Income: 25,000 % 22.5p = £5,625

Pretty grim, eh? It gets worse.

From this sum, you've got to pay your manager 20 per cent, which slices off another £1,125. Now you've only got £4,500. That might buy you the insurance for your pink Porsche.

'It's also worth remembering that any single needs a video,' says Dave Clark. 'MTV, other music channels and television shows drive the singles market, and even a cheap but quality video that might get accepted by MTV will cost ten thousand pounds. Usually, you pay for half of that. Your share is added to your overall debt with the record company.'

So, if you insist on flying to the Bahamas and shipping out that white Rolls-Royce to use in your video, think how long it will take you to recover those sums if you are getting only 22.5p per single sold.

These figures make grim reading enough for artists who are prudent with the slices of cash they do finally get. If you are an artist who drinks it away (or, worse, spares no expense with the high life and saves nothing for tax), you are about to fall into a serious black hole.

Of course, this is a harsh picture. Some videos relaunch bands and pay themselves back in other ways. When Backstreet Boys released the single and video of 'Backstreet's Back', the cost for the video alone was rumoured to be $850,000. Fortunately, that single classic pop promo relaunched the band and they went on to release one of the music world's biggest-selling albums ever, *Millennium*. By then, that costly video was worth every penny. There has to be some logic to spending such sums, otherwise artists would never make videos. I am just trying to take a little of the romantic sheen off these matters.

Also, good singles sell albums and it's from albums that you can make a lot of money. Artists whose albums maybe never hit the top spot but stay in the top twenty for months, sometimes longer, are making vast amounts of money. Those who enter at number one and then plummet out of sight might not even see any profit at all (although some contracts allow for a bonus if an artist reaches a number-one slot).

However, even if you have singles and albums flying out of the shops and are doing really well, the record company will still need to recoup their total advance – in our example, £250,000 – from this income before you see any more money. They account twice a year and so you may not see any of that money for many months, even years. Also, most record companies do not have an obligation to send you financial paperwork until you have recouped your advance, but by that stage you may have toured the world, worked exceptionally hard for two years and come home to find a zero balance. If you do, you will scream 'rip-off!' – but it isn't anything of the sort. The chances are it is because you did not take the necessary steps at the initial stage.

You might be saying, 'Why do I need to know all this when I haven't even got a record deal?' The answer is that hopefully you will soon be in a position where people are talking to you about these matters. As with your choice of manager and other personnel, decisions you make at such an early stage could adversely affect your income, control and artistic freedom for the rest of your career. Also, if you win the next series of *Pop Idol* – and I sincerely hope you do – then this chapter is even more important, because at that level a mistake that might cost you 20 per cent of your earnings is a hell of a lot more painful.

Dave Clark sees many bands failing to lay the foundations.

The problem is, when the initial record deal is for a fifteen-thousand-pound advance, no artist wants to pay accountants, lawyers, managers. They just think that the money is too small to justify it. If that artist becomes successful and the income is suddenly on a different level, none of that initial planning has been done and it will come back to haunt them. I see it so many times and, more often than not, you can trace back problems to early decisions that were – or weren't – made.

At the same time, you need to be pragmatic. You are an unsigned act and you have somehow managed to solicit interest from a record company. You are offered a deal. Unless you are one of the lucky few acts – and we are talking a handful each year – then you will not be in much of a position to bargain for your first record contract. A good lawyer will be able to help, and so will a meticulous accountant, but the balance of power is not in your favour. To put it bluntly, beggars can't be choosers.

However, many industry lawyers will quickly advise you to walk away from any contract that is unduly onerous on you. If this happens to you, don't be disappointed about what might have been – if the contract is a con, then all you have missed out on is years and years of very hard graft for little or no financial reward. Dave Clark explains, 'Many young unsigned artists may not have a chance. They will be told these are industry norms and it may be a take-it-or-leave-it situation. There are plenty of other artists out there who would agree to those terms.' If this happens to you and you decide to take the gamble, you may be able to renegotiate two or three albums down the path, and only then if other record labels are sniffing around, too.

Of course, many rock and pop stars make phenomenal amounts of money – or seem to. We've all seen the headlines in the newspapers: 'New band signs £1 million deal'. Using my approximate formula above, if there are four members of the band and the income has to last them three years, they might each see about £100,000 net, after the deductions that I explained above. Not bad, but not the Lotto.

'What about Gareth Gates?' I hear you cry. 'He earned three and a half million pounds in one year!' Admittedly, there are not many teenage kids with that kind of money, even if it might have to last them for three years. But get this: there are even fewer teenagers who will get signed for figures like these. The music business of today is in a state of flux and huge advances are confined to the very highest-profile artists, usually with an extensive career already behind them. Forget conversations about Robbie Williams signing for £75 million. This is not the stage you are at. Many first-time record deals may offer you £100,000, maybe £200,000 advances, but many more will be a lot less.

The sums are smaller than you think and so are the number of record deals available. Tony Wadsworth, president of EMI says,

A company like Parlophone, which is the biggest of our labels, would probably not sign more than three or four album deals in a year. There would be a few single deals, but ultimately in order to make them into album deals. If we sign someone to a record deal, we see that as a major commitment not just from us for money, but from the artist who is entrusting you with a part of their livelihood. Many labels take the attitude that 'if you throw so much crap against the wall, some of it will stick', which is an irresponsible attitude and one that is becoming decreasingly feasible in the modern climate.

You might read this section and still be thinking, 'Well, Noel Gallagher's loaded.' Noel Gallagher has sold *millions and millions* of albums and, in Marcus Russell, has one of the top managers in the music industry. During a court case against a former manager, Elton John was famously asked to list his extravagant lifestyle, revealing he spent tens of thousands of pounds in one year on flowers. But Elton John has been a working musician since the early 1970s and with his success globally has sold in excess of 150 million records. Even squeaky-clean Sir Cliff Richard, whom you may not aspire to follow in any way, has a substantial property portfolio, rumoured to have been started way back in the very early 1960s with some of his first royalty cheques. These are not just great performers: they are more often than not shrewd businessmen or, at the very least, know how to spot and employ shrewd businessmen.

Natalie Appleton says,

It can be tough if you are naïve. I learned the hard way through being naïve in this business, but at such an early age you can't know what you are getting into. The whole business side can be fraught with problems. It is a really bad business! Singing and performing live is a great high but the other side of music is very corrupt. You have to be very, very careful not to sign your life away.

Finally, a word in defence of the record companies. The above advice is weighted in your favour, hopefully to help you avoid some of the less scrupulous record executives out there. You should also know that the majority of the record companies are not sharks, they are not crooks, they are not trying to rip you off. They have a business to run and try to do so as profitably as possible. They are simply looking out for their interests just as you should look out for yours. Many pop and rock stars demonise record companies and there have been many high-profile spats. But don't tar them all with the same brush. Just make sure you go into any contract with your eyes wide open.

A PUBLISHING CONTRACT
Music publishers come along and pick up their income from the record company and other exploitation of your works. The copyright belongs to you until you sell it to a publishing company and they will then collect money on your behalf. This may be less important initially than the recording contract, but in your later career it can be an invaluable source of extra income.

A songwriter will get more of the publishing money than other band members. This can often be a source of great friction, because, if there are five members of a band who have just toured the world for year and one member is getting substantially more money than the other four, that can cause problems. There are several famous examples of bands, such as U2 and the Strokes, who split all income equally, regardless of who writes the material and who is viewed as more important creatively.

OTHER INCOME SOURCES
Pop artists are often offered lucrative deals by third parties who want to be associated with their image. Depending on your opinion of such deals, Dave Clark says pop artists in particular can do very well out of agreements that are unrelated to recording and the music.

> Obviously artists like the Prodigy shun endorsement deals for hair products for example, but pop stars can do these sponsorship deals with little or no effect on their credibility and quite often with a very positive effect on record sales. In addition, there is always a very positive effect on their bank balance, not least because these sometimes large lump sums are sizeable one-off payments.

SOME PROBLEMS TO AVOID
Watch out for hangers-on. Sometimes it seems that everybody wants to rip pop stars off. And I mean everybody. You see entourages, extra studio people with no apparent purpose, builders, all sorts. Some people see pop stars as a cash cow. You have got to be aware of that.

Even if you sign a well-negotiated record deal and are starting to enjoy the financial benefits of a successful chart career, you still need to be careful. One thing that can drag many pop stars into financial difficulty is their desire to be seen to be living the pop-star life. There is a huge expectation on pop stars to *live* like pop stars – from themselves, their friends, the media and their peer group.

Your accountant will see the end result only when bank statements come through, most worryingly with huge amounts of 'cash' being drawn. Other items come up such as limos, luxury hotels. Drugs can burn up literally thousands of pounds in a matter of days. These are just the financial repercussions. With stars who are wise and can afford this lifestyle, it is understandable that they want to enjoy their money. Bloody hell, I would.

But don't enjoy it before you've got it, or, worse still, if you haven't got it at all. Dave Clark says,

> If you are a young artist and not used to having money, please, please, please take great care. This is your business, you sell records, you have to run it commercially. I can spot the stars who don't listen to that advice a mile off. They have nothing. Some of them might technically be bankrupt yet headlining major festivals.

You see those pop stars photographed in *Heat* magazine falling out of a central London nightclub, taking their bottle of champagne into their waiting limo, being whisked off with friends to another party before crashing at a top hotel with all the trimmings. Sounds familiar? Well, a good number of these people have got less money than you and would certainly not be their bank manager's favourite customer. Fact.

What we've looked at so for is a mere sliver of information on a subject that people study for years to master. I am not suggesting for one minute that you become a qualified accountant and understand every single stream of income in your career to the nearest penny. You should employ a top accountant like Dave Clark for that express purpose. There are many books on the market that delve into these issues in much greater depth, and if you feel suitably inspired to get your hands dirty then they are worth a look. Nonetheless, hopefully this section will have given you a fresh view on certain issues to look out for and will leave you better equipped to work hard, play hard and enjoy the benefits of both.

THE LEGALITIES OF BEING A POP STAR

Louis Walsh has this sound advice:

> The most important thing for any young hopeful is to get a good lawyer, and an established music lawyer at that. They need to know about record labels, who is hot, who is not and so on. Your lawyer is almost as important to you as your manager or record company. He needs to be above board, give you time and see the big picture – and already represent at least three or four class acts.

The problem is, we all know what legal advice means – cost. 'Legal bills will hurt,' says Stephen Barnes of Upshot Promotions, 'but look at it as insurance.' He continues,

> If your music and career are precious you need to protect them. Music-business lawyers are also good sources of talent, too, so it won't hurt befriending a known music-business firm. They are invariably very well connected and can be vitally helpful. Most will give you a little bit of time for free. Make your position clear about money and if they believe in you they will work with you.

With this in mind, one of the country's top music-business law firms, Davenport Lyons, have prepared this summary of the major issues you need to be aware of when trying to secure a career in the music business. This section is necessarily very matter-of-fact. After all, conversations with lawyers are not the ones in which you crack jokes about falling out of a tour bus with no pants on. As with the advice above on money and music, if you find this legal talk boring and choose to ignore it, you are a fool.

THE RECORD CONTRACT

Rupert Sprawson writes: Most companies have a 'standard' form of contract, but, depending on the bargaining power of the artist, there may be some concessions given on certain points. The key areas of recording contract can be broken down as follows:

ADVANCE

In the majority of cases an artist will be advanced a sum of money, which will keep the artist housed and fed while they are recording their first album or single. In determining the level of advance the record company will make a calculation as to what future record sales might be. Any sums advanced to an artist by the record company will generally be recouped against all record sales.

Because of the often large sums of money spent on recording albums and videos, it may be many years before an advance is recouped. Only a very few artists ever have the luxury of actually receiving royalty payments.

EXCLUSIVITY

The vast majority of record deals are exclusive, which means an artist cannot record for other companies – that goes for both albums and videos. There are limited exceptions to this, though, and record companies generally allow artists to perform as nonfeatured session musicians and do production work for others.

TERRITORY

It is common for major record companies to sign artists exclusively for the world. However, where there is considerable competition to sign a band it is sometimes possible to exclude territories from the deal, leaving the band to sign to other companies in other territories.

TERM

In the world of guitar bands it is common for there to be an initial commitment to one album with options exercisable by a record company for up to another five. This means that, after release of the first album, the company can either drop the band or, if the first album has performed well, continue with their investment by asking for another album.

OWNERSHIP

Artists pay for their own recordings through the record company's recouping of the artists' advances from royalties, but the record company get to own any recordings made by them usually for the full period of copyright (currently this is fifty years from the end of the year in which a recording is made or, if during that period it is released, fifty years from the end of the year in which the recording is released).

RELEASE COMMITMENT

It is common nowadays to include an obligation on a record company to release an album or single within a specific period of time after delivery, usually three to six months. 'Delivery' takes place when a record company confirms that a recording is commercially, technically and artistically satisfactory.

COSTS AND RECOUPING
Generally all sums advanced by a record company are recoupable from an artist's royalty. Typically, sums advanced will include all recording and video costs, tour support costs and website-development costs.

LEAVING-MEMBER CLAUSES
Where there more artists than one contracting with a label, as part of a band, for instance, it is common to have a clause that protects the company's investment when a band disbands or a member quits.

CREATIVE ISSUES
It is important for a band to retain as much control as possible over issues such as choice of producer, recording budget, studio, song selection, remixers, artwork, website content and exploitation of sound recordings other than by way of record sales, for example, licences for the use of recordings in film or TV and licences for sample usage. In practice, this is difficult to achieve and a record company seeking to protect its investment and maintain absolute control over the recording process will be unwilling to concede anything more than consultation rights with the artist.

INTERNET
To protect their interests, record companies often try to retain ownership rights over an artist's domain name as well as the fan database and all website content.

MERCHANDISING
Occasionally record companies try to retain the right to use an artist's name and image for the purposes of merchandising, endorsement and sponsorship. Thankfully, this is rare nowadays and any attempt to retain control over these rights must be fiercely resisted by the artist.

ARTIST SOCIETIES
Apart from the Musicians' Union UK, performers' interests are represented by the Association of United Recording Artists (AURA) and

Performing Artists' Media Rights Association (PAMRA). PAMRA membership tends to consist of nonfeatured and session artists, while AURA champions the interests of featured artists. Both organisations collect and distribute the performers' share of sound-recording, public-performance and broadcast income, which in the UK is collected by Phonographic Performance Limited, or PPL. Performers have been entitled to share in this income since 1996. This means that an artist is entitled to a payment every time recordings embodying his or her performances are broadcast on TV, radio, clubs and other live venues.

© Rupert Sprawson, Davenport Lyons, 2002

There are, of course, hundreds of other possible issues to look out for and pitfalls to avoid, controlled-composition clauses and suchlike, but this book is not the place to advise you of those. What this chapter has done is set out the basic points that will crop up in any reputable record contract. If you have found any of this financial and legal information difficult to follow, sit down with your parents or a friend and go over it all again. Keep trying. If you can understand the basics, then you are arming yourself with a highly valuable tool in looking after your business.

If you are worried about the costs of dealing with lawyers and accountants, fear not. Albert Samuel of Mission Control, who, as we've seen, manages So Solid Crew, has this simple but sage advice:

> Most quality lawyers (and accountants) are very long-term. Therefore you lose nothing as an individual by phoning them up and saying, 'I am starting out, I haven't got any money but there is someone interested in me. Can I come and talk to you?' This industry will only survive by looking long-term and seeing the bigger picture. If all he is concerned about is his immediate billing to you, then maybe he is not the right lawyer (or accountant) for you.

Finally, for both financial and legal issues, there is but one simple and cast-iron tip: get good professional advice, the best you can realistically afford. At rates that can run to several hundred pounds an hour, these professionals can be intimidating to meet and deal with. Don't be frightened by this. The fact that you are bothering to seek good advice means you are already taking your career very seriously.

For that you should be congratulated.

12. ALTERNATIVE ROUTES TO FAME

'He gave us some good career tips. He said, "So you want to get into the music business? Good luck. They'll never let you work on your tan."'
Nash Kato of Urge Overkill, recalling advice from Neil Diamond

Unfortunately, for some of you, major record deals may well be about as likely as that *Popstars* reject, Darius Danesh, getting to number one. Er, sorry, bad example. Put it another way, record deals are like the proverbial hens' teeth. However, just because all your efforts to secure a contract are fruitless, it doesn't mean you cannot still be a pop star.

I'm sure you've read numerous stories about bedroom boffins who decide one day to write a song, sit up into the small hours twiddling with their hard drives and end up the next day with a song that within weeks is sitting on top of the charts. It seems such an attractive proposition. None of that messy live work, no need to humiliate yourself in front of a panel of audition judges – just quick, easy pop success from the comfort of your own home. Sort of like convenience stardom.

By this point in the book, you should know better than that. Self-recording and self-releasing your records is a genuinely viable alternative to the more traditional paths to success we've looked at so far. However, as with every other aspect of pop stardom, it is not an easy option.

With the power of modern technology, self-produced albums are indeed a perfectly viable option. It has been a tool that the more ingenious artists have used for many years, long before the capacity of computers turned a bedroom into a studio. A few years ago, there was a news headline saying more DJ decks had been sold than guitars. In the new millennium, computers and music software are outselling guitars.

Let's take as an example Daniel Bedingfield. He wrote his debut single and UK number-one hit 'Gotta Get Through This' in his bedroom using a computer and microphone that cost less than £1,000. The tune became an underground hit on the Ayia Napa club scene before topping the charts in late 2001. By the autumn of 2002, he was perched at number one in the American singles charts. So it can and does happen.

Think about that story, though. Did Daniel have no prior knowledge of making music technically, no writing skills whatsoever, no contacts in the club underground and no drive to make this happen? Of course not. His song didn't just float out of his bedroom window and across the night skies on to the dance floors of Ayia Napa.

A more extreme example of self-recording is Stephen Jones, an artist who began his career with no fewer than five albums in one nine-month spell. Under the band name of Babybird, Stephen went on to enjoy a number-three hit single with the darkly seductive 'You're Gorgeous', a song that enjoyed major radio play despite being essentially about using sex to sell products. He also secured a top-ten gold album and eight other top-forty singles. This was the culmination of years of work for Stephen, who had actually found his way into music indirectly through performance art. In alternative theatre he directed, acted and then wrote soundtracks, funded by the Arts Council and Barclays Bank (for more on funding your career, see Chapter 14). At this stage he was something of a technophobe and remains defiantly so to this day.

However, his decision to release those five self-financed albums was a unique and ingenious ploy that catapulted him into a high-profile music career. It is worth remembering that Stephen remains one of the music industry's most prolific songwriters, so perhaps you should set your sights lower than the four hundred original songs he had already composed when he started recording these DIY records! Stephen says,

> My tapes were being played by Graham Wench, who booked bands at Sheffield Leadmill, but people must have liked them because they were being nicked. Dave Taylor, who ran the legendary Fon Studios, hatched a plan with Graham one night to put out five albums of my material in just nine months. I wasn't even there when they thought of this, but the idea stuck in the morning haze.'
>
> Dave funded the first album, *I Was Born a Man*, himself so he was therefore essential to kick-starting my career. He became my manager after that. Prior to this, Dave had hawked my demos round London with no success. No one took my work seriously for two years. Suddenly, with the self-financed albums, people who had thrown the demo cassettes in the bin were now very interested.

Stephen still finds this solitary approach to recording works for him.

Recording music alone gives you complete control. I was either too intimidated or self-conscious in front of even one person. I will always work alone with my own equipment in my own space, as it's quicker to get it right and there are no rules. Then I will go into a larger studio with the right people to flesh it out.

If this is a route to success that appeals to you, Stephen suggests that having the latest state-of-the-art gear is not necessarily a passport to success. Indeed, he feels that a more Spartan setup can be more fruitful.

I've always loved film scores with big strings, so my task when I first started was to take dreadful synthesiser sounds, twist them through effects and make it sound like a sixty-piece orchestra.

I have never read a manual. I just get equipment an idiot could use and, through a series of mistakes and happy accidents, I get there. Mistakes are good. I also advise you keep it simple. I still use four- and eight-track recorders because it makes you more resourceful and selective. You don't just add loads of tracks just for the sake of it.

Nonetheless, despite being a huge fan of home recording, he does value certain elements of a musical education. 'The only thing I regret a little is not remembering the music stuff I was taught at school,' he admits. 'Even though all my music is based on simplicity, I don't know any chords. I do wish I could remember how to play the piano and guitar better.'

BASIC RECORDING EQUIPMENT

Whether you're a singer or a band, you should invest in a cheap four-track tape recorder. This way you'll be able to record the basics of your music (you can usually squeeze at least six tracks on to a four-track machine without losing too much quality) or practise vocal harmonising with yourself or your band mates easily, cheaply and away from the expensive professional studio. A basic machine from TASCAM will cost from a little over £100, or can be picked up second-hand for less. As Daniel Bedingfield proved, a fairly basic computer setup with the right sort of software can have equally effective results.

You should not, however, make the assumption that you can 'buy' good songs through expensive equipment. Liam Howlett of the Prodigy has even reduced the amount of home studio gear he uses. The basic principles of how he records his material have barely changed from his first home demo (see Chapter 6).

A few years ago [says Liam], I stripped my home studio right back to basics. The main core of what I do is the source of the sounds. I love the old analogue keyboards from the 1970s and 1980s, old Korg and Moog keyboards that you can't buy any more and can't reproduce digitally. The sound source has to be analogue for me. I had got swept into buying too much gear. If you do start to earn money, you need to be really headstrong not to fall into that trap. People always go overboard with more equipment than they need. I could have spent much less looking back on it.

The only thing that has changed from my first demos and 'Firestarter', for example, is basically how it is sequenced together. My computer makes it much tighter and uses less tracks. Whereas before my old Roland W30 might fill up sixteen tracks really quickly and the keyboard would start to f*** up. Apart from that, my sounds, where I source that and my ideas from are the same as when I started. It is all still a home studio to be honest.

Liam suggests that even pop acts can use this technology.

I think anyone can record at home, I really believe that. With a budget of five thousand pounds, I could set you up a recording studio at home and be recording Will Young and it would sound like chart quality to the average person when it's played on the radio. For kids who have a lot less than that, you can still get some fantastic home recording equipment. All you really need to get going is your computer – you can get everything you need from that. Maybe some speakers, too, but you don't need to spend more than a thousand pounds.

Also, don't be fooled that a big studio can necessarily improve your sound. I recorded 'Minefields' on *The Fat of the Land* album on my home gear and then took it to a top London studio. We spent hours on it and kept referring back to my original demo. That original demo would just jump out of the speakers, so we ended up using that on the album. Same vein with 'Smack My

Bitch Up' with how the bottom end of the sonics are so huge. There was no specific reason for it to be such a big sound, but that is the way it came out in my home studio on that particular day. I was twiddling around and fell across that.

GETTING YOUR RECORD OUT THERE

If you are pursuing the self-recording route, you will need to wear many different hats. In particular, you will be relying on yourself and your contacts to get your record out to the public. This is not something that should be undertaken lightly, otherwise your efforts will be wasted.

My old band the Chocolate Speedway Riders 'self-distributed' their debut single, which meant we managed to strong-arm one solitary copy into Tower Records in Piccadilly Circus on sale-or-return. Four weeks later we went back and, rather predictably but no less disappointingly, were asked to remove that sole copy, dog-eared, worthless and unwanted. Pointless.

Damian Harris of Skint Records was rather more adept at distributing his output: 'I'd worked in a record shop and for Loaded records and I did have some experience,' he says. 'I had contacts with pressing plants and record distributors, so to a degree I was advantaged, but only because I had worked hard to get those contacts.'

Another band who recorded their own material in order to gain the exposure and groundswell of following needed to succeed are So Solid Crew. They already had a healthy profile and underground presence before they signed a major-label deal or even prior to the involvement of their manager Albert Samuel. They had been cutting self-financed white labels and even ran two of their own record labels, So Solid Beats and Paper Money Recordings. They would often put their members into the studio, cut dub plates then take those records to the pirate stations involved in their scene, various DJs and shops. This is not an easy challenge, as Albert explains.

They had got off their butts and done it themselves. That requires no small amount of vision, a lot of belief and having the courage of your convictions to finance it. It was the same with Oxide and Neutrino. They pressed up several thousand copies of 'Bound for the Reload' at their own expense and got the underground buzzing before they'd even approached, or been approached by, established companies.

LICENSING DEALS

Stuart David of Looper feels that the Holy Grail of securing a record contract need not actually be your sole target, especially in light of the changing dynamics within the record industry.

> The extent to which bands and artists need to follow the traditional route laid down by record companies has changed drastically in the last few years. In the past, if you wanted to make a record, you pretty much needed a record company, but that's no longer the case. Every year the quality of what you can do on your own equipment goes up and every year the price comes down.
>
> I'd recommend spending some time looking at the possibilities of what you can do on a PC or Mac. It's no longer the case that computers are limited to being suitable just for electronic music. You'll get the same quality on a home computer as in many professional studios if you know what you're doing, on everything from a five-piece guitar band right up to a full orchestral arrangement.

He is also refreshingly optimistic and encouraging about your next step.

> When your record's completed, you have two main options: a record contract or a licensing deal. You'll find that getting a licensing deal is not nearly as hard as getting a full record deal, because it's not as big a risk for the record company. They don't have to take such a big gamble because they don't have to pay out a huge amount of money to record your album, since you've already made it. They also don't have to face any uncertainty about whether they're going to be happy with your finished record and hopeful about its commercial potential, because they can hear it in advance.

> This all sounds very rosy, but surely the licensing deal is far inferior to a standard record contract, isn't it? Not necessarily. You might not get the big advance (which may well not come with an orthodox record deal, anyway) and your friends might not get as excited when you rush into the pub and say, 'I've just signed my first licensing deal!' However, from your point of view, having a licensing deal can often be much the same as having a record deal. Stuart says there's also one big advantage.

You'll get exactly the same promotion, distribution, royalty as you would on a most starter record deals, but after a certain period – say five or ten years – the ownership of the record reverts back to you again, leaving you free to license it to someone else or even back to the same company. If the record's done well over that period you'll probably be able to negotiate much better terms for yourself than you initially had on it too.

A third option when you've made your finished album is to bypass record companies completely and look for a deal directly with a distributor. Stuart says that, in some cases, that might be even easier to find than a deal with a record company, but not that different.

With a lot of these deals, they'll give you an advance to cover your pressing and printing costs, they do some advertising for their releases, but effectively you are your own record company, so you get the main share of the profits. It's not all straightforward, though: you'll probably have to employ your own PR company to cover the press for you if you don't want to do that yourself but, again, the distribution company might advance you the money for that. It'll be a bit more work than a licensing deal, and you'll have to co-ordinate the whole campaign – so, if you don't want to get too involved in that side of things, a licensing deal is probably better. Either is a perfectly valid alternative to the traditional route of a record deal.

It is easy to dismiss these options. Let's face it, I'd much rather get signed by a major label and earn a million-pound advance and a headline in the *Sun*. Wouldn't we all? I'd also like to have a Ferrari, more hair, less belly and the looks of Brad Pitt. But you can't have everything in life.

Don't underestimate the long-term benefits of self-recording, either. It is not necessarily the poorer option or a short-term plan taken by those who can't get record deals. Far from it. Signing a major record deal too soon can kill a talent overnight rather than make it. In the process, working on your own records means you learn so much about the industry, studios, costs, distribution, schedules and so forth. Thus, when you finally get to talk to that major-label president who loves your talent more than life itself, you will be all the more knowledgeable and able to secure the right deal for you, rather than just any deal.

13. SUPERSTAR DJ

'There's a thin line between what's hip and what's unhip. I like to walk that line.' Stephen Bishop

In recent years, the role of the DJ has morphed into one of a celebrity high-roller, jetting through the air to play a two-hour set in Ibiza for £20,000, working with huge rock acts for dance remixes, being worshipped at the altar of superclubs and quite often mutating into a recording artist in his or her own right. Of course, it wasn't always this way. Sure, we had Tony Blackburn and cutting-edge pirate stations such as Radio Caroline in the 1960s. We've always had John Peel (thankfully), and high-profile DJs have always been part of the celebrity crowd. But club DJ-ing was never like this. Whatever happened to 'The Birdy Song' and snatches of the occasional Elvis classics? Where are the much-loved, mistimed introductions such as 'Here's the best disco song you've ever . . . no, er, yup, here it comes . . .'? Give me those deep-voiced enticements to 'Show your lady friend just how much you love her . . .' Of course, I am exaggerating. Underground DJ-ing has always been about innovation and musical discovery, but nevertheless the final years of the 1990s witnessed the commercial zenith of the so-called superstar DJ.

For exactly this reason, DJ-ing is now perceived as a bona fide celebrity occupation in its own right. The naïve among you who have been a little daunted by the previous chapters and the hard work needed to be a pop star will perhaps be pondering how great it must be to spin a few records – not even your own – and get paid big bucks for the pleasure. OK, time for another reality check.

Being a 'superstar DJ' is as hard as, if not harder than, breaking into the pop business. It will almost certainly take you longer, possibly a *lot* longer. If you want a quick DJ buck, start making yourself available for weddings and eighteenth-birthday parties.

In Chapter 16 you can read a little about the wealth of musical influences out there for you. Let me tell you this: famous DJs are *without exception* musical archivists – no, archaeologists – boasting encyclopedic knowledge of the most obscure reference points from decades of music. They can instantly dig up a five-second sample out of some unknown hip-hop B-side or trace the roots of a song that you thought was brand-new, back through a complex and diverse musical ancestry. They have record collections that can run into tens of thousands. They live, breathe and eat music. These are the people you want on your pub quiz team.

Bearing all that in mind, how might you become a superstar DJ? I asked Damian Harris, owner of Skint Records, which is home to arguably the world's most famous DJ, Fatboy Slim, a.k.a. Norman Cook (some people will argue Paul Oakenfold is the world's most famous DJ, so we'll talk to him in a moment). Damian is prodigiously talented – when Fatboy's album *You've Come a Long Way Baby* hit number one across the world in 1999, selling more than 7 million copies, Damian was not yet into his thirties. Damian is also a renowned DJ and records as an artist himself under the nom de plume 'the Midfield General'.

His views on Fatboy's and his own success in the club world offer an intriguing insight into the challenges facing any aspiring DJ.

Norman obviously had a very healthy recording career before Fatboy Slim, but he was never really known as a DJ. He had always toured with bands, but it was actually his DJ-ing that broke him beyond that and you can learn a lot from looking at what he has done. He had all the elements in place to get to where he is now, making great music that he wanted to play at the Boutique club [run by Damian]. All his best tunes were made on a Sunday after a heavy Saturday night – the night before was always his inspiration.

Fatboy is very prolific. He's always got something on the go and has a very broad diversity of influences. He seemed to be able to turn to any style but with his own unique stamp, so you can learn from that, too. He's constantly working and writing and you can do that, too – you don't need to be signed. Also, I liked a lot of his earlier music but not all of it, so be conscious that you can and will make mistakes, but if you keep working you will get there. Ironically, with Norman, it was only once he really didn't care about making hits that he started actually having huge hits. You can try too hard at any level.

How do I go about getting my music to people in the club world? Is it the same process as trying to get a record deal?

Realistically, sending a mix to a big-name club and getting noticed is highly unlikely. My own demo box is always overspilling. It's virtually impossible for you to get noticed through that route. Instead, you should try to do your own thing. Try working at bars – I played wherever I could. Be patient because it is a long slog. I started when I was fifteen and at that point a DJ was not a role that was perceived as glamorously as it is in the modern era. I had to take what work I could to progress and learn – parties, bars, clubs, whatever. I came to Brighton when I was nineteen after I had reached the pinnacle of DJ-ing in my local area near Canterbury.

Once in Brighton I started again almost from scratch, really, working hard, building a reputation, getting my name known. I got a job doing the backroom at the Coco Club. Then I got a warm-up in the main room, which led to a slot for me when the main DJ was absent and so on. You do need that slice of luck but you need to create the opportunity for the luck to happen. If you're not out there playing, you won't get any lucky breaks. Get out there. Do mix tapes for people. You should be in that super-enthusiastic stage, wanting to do tapes every single day. It's no good sitting in your bedroom bemoaning the fact no one understands your genius.

Damian's biggest piece of advice is to start your own club.

Being associated with a great club, like the Boutique, is helpful. People are saying there's a recession in dance music and, yes, it is very hard to break into it. But don't get stressed out by all that talk. Get your friends together, get your club started, do it yourself – you have a much better chance. My first gigs were at the Whitstable Labour Club in their function room. I also did stuff in the local art centre. So scour your area and find a good venue. Talk to the owner and put your own night on – the owners want the club full and the bar busy. Try colleges, hotels wherever – use your initiative.

Once you've got the club, you can play your own music, talk to like-minded people and get a buzz going. Your progress and popularity will boil down to your choice of records, your style and whether you've got the X-factor. It's all about your opinion at that stage and that will make or break you. Big Beats Boutique was all about playing new records and we built our reputation such that people expected the unexpected, they enjoyed the unpredictability of that.

Once you've got your club going, you can start meeting people from other clubs and start networking. We built many fruitful and lasting friendships. For example, we saw the Heavenly Social in London, which inspired certain ideas in us for our club. We established relations with them. Then, with the Chemical Brothers, we built our network and all sorts of things started to happen. We invited Heavenly Social to play at the Boutique; they reciprocated with their club and we moved forward. Thrive off each other.

Damian's own career as the Midfield General offers many good pointers to aspiring DJs and remixers.

I used a pseudonym because it was a good excuse for a nickname! It was all about learning initially. I had a few records out but did a lot of remixes, too. I learned about studio work, worked with vocals on remixes for free just to get the opportunity. I learned how a record sounds in a club when you've mixed it right or wrong. All those elements only come with time. Once I had enough material and enough of a name established (which took years) it was time to record an album.

Damian encourages hopefuls not to be intimidated if they spot a celebrity DJ at a club.

If you see known players in the market, go up to them politely and give them a tape. If someone is demanding or aggressive when they come up to me, I won't take the tape. I don't mind being approached – that's part of my job. That kid giving me his tape in a club might just be the next Fatboy Slim.

One core aspect of the pop business need not be such a concern for wannabe DJs, suggests Damian.

Personally, I don't ask for a photo – it makes no difference to me at all. A lot of DJs I know loved nightclubs but couldn't dance and felt very awkward. Instead they got behind the decks as a way around that awkwardness. How they look is irrelevant. Look at Fatboy's videos – he's hardly ever in them!

As we've seen, Damian is regarded as a prodigiously young music impresario, yet he warns against expecting too much too soon.

The dance genre tends to be full of very experienced players. Their knowledge and years of experience are seen as a positive, unlike the pop genre, where youth is king. Look at all the top DJs: they are in their thirties mainly; they've been doing it for years and years. On occasion I actually get people saying to me, 'I want the DJ lifestyle,' but that's just so misguided. The question any aspiring DJ needs to ask themselves is this: is music your all-encompassing passion; do you think about it all day, every day? Is it the energy from the records and the music you desire or the tabloid profile and first-class flights? If it is the latter, think again. Even if you are absolutely superb and a unique talent it could be fifteen years before you start to get anywhere. Being a DJ is not the quick route to fame.

Another superstar DJ who has successfully enjoyed a recording career as an artist in tandem with his club profile is Paul Oakenfold. He is undoubtedly one of the world's premier DJs and is certainly one of the crucial figures in the relentless rise of club culture. His story is a fine example of perseverance and thinking laterally. He found that his early career was problematic in terms of getting help.

I created my own break. No one would give me a break as a DJ, so I started running my own club night. Then no one would give me a job in a record company, so I started taking underground records from England directly to America, trying to do a US deal for that record and earning myself a finder's fee. I found the UK record industry obstructive early on – it can be difficult to get into.

He recommends pressing up white labels if you can afford them, but to avoid causing unnecessary financial burden. He also thinks that you should think twice before playing clubs for the sake of it.

It's not the number of gigs you play, rather more a case of playing the *right* gigs. Less is more in my opinion. Do the right things rather than a lot of things. You can help yourself by getting to know local promoters and, later, promoters at bigger clubs. Hang out with some of them, go to their clubs and let them know what you do and how you do it.

His success as a DJ, remixer and producer led him on to his own artist album with 2002's *Bunka*, but this progress was no overnight success. 'For the past ten years I'd been creating music under various different names,' he says, 'but I was never comfortable with putting out an Oakenfold record. It was, however, an idea that I'd been thinking about for a long time and eventually I felt it was time to make that record.'

Paul's considered approach may not be the swift route to fame that you are looking for, but bear in mind he has in the meantime worked with some of the world's top artists – Madonna, U2, Snoop Dogg, Happy Mondays, New Order, the Cure and Massive Attack. His rise to chart success as an artist in his own right is a good example of how an aspiring DJ or studio whiz can sometimes make that crossover. It is also a fine example of how sometimes an artist can break through into the music business from less orthodox avenues.

Paul Oakenfold's career began in London at the end of the 1970s, as he worked in small clubs around the West End. Oakenfold's rising reputation led to a job as an A & R man at the UK-based Champion Records, where his first signing was Will Smith, his second was Salt 'n' Pepa. Oakenfold was among the first DJs to start regular club sessions on the Spanish island of Ibiza, leading to a new sound in dance music and the now annual pilgrimage of European youth to the island each summer. In 1990, he started his own record label, Perfecto which is home to such European DJ talents as Timo Maas and Hernan Cattaneo.

Peruse Oakenfold's lengthy career and you will see hundreds of late nights working, thousands of conversations spent networking and getting his face known, countless air miles on the way to working in scores of studios with hundreds of acts. It may seem daunting that you are at the wrong end of this exhausting journey, but it is better that you know now what is involved. If you are not in this for the long haul, you are better not to start the journey at all.

Working as a DJ can sometimes open up other avenues than the ones you expect. Liam Howlett started off as a teenage hip-hop DJ, and that laid the foundations for his career as the Prodigy, one of the world's biggest bands. His story started in DJ-ing but diverted into another genre shortly after.

My very first demo did not have my own music. I'd been f***ing around more as a scratch DJ. I was very young, excited by Grandmaster Flash and the hip-hop scene. I was doing lots of pause-button mixing, that sort of thing. At fifteen, I entered a mixing competition on Mike Allen's *Capital Radio Hip-hop Show*, sending in two mixes under two different names. I'd borrowed my mate's four-track Portastudio – it was the most basic way of recording, I guess. It was very time-consuming.

I remember with records that might have a two-second break, if I was trying to extend that I would be spinning one record on one track, then spinning another on another track. These days that can be done in two seconds on a sampler. Listening back to that mix now, I think 'So what?' – but at the time it was pretty cool.

I'd sent the first mix in but a couple of weeks later I'd decided it was shit, so I did another one and sent that in, too. I came first and third. That really gave me a boost. I thought, 'Yes, I can do this.'

Liam's interest in DJ-ing and hip-hop soon led him on to the next stage of his career.

I hooked up with a bunch of DJs and emcees from Essex. We were just f***ing around with this four-track, recording demos. We shipped this demo around to record companies but we didn't have much luck, probably because we were shit. Actually, to be fair, the music was cool, the ideas were there. This was still all lots of loops and samples, not original material as such, but we were having fun. Our goal was to put on these parties for all our mates and play our own music and do it live.

When the hip-hop outfit eventually came to nothing, Liam stayed focused. 'I worked at a building site one summer and saved up to buy a Roland W30 keyboard. At that point, it all really started for me.' (See also Chapter 6.)

Here's one final piece of advice about this marketplace. If you do slip into the club world and start creating your own material, you need to be aware of a slightly different dynamic of this genre. The market is driven by singles and many record companies in this sphere just sign one-off songs. You may well be offered a deal, which will no doubt be hugely exciting. It is more probable than an eight-album pop contract, simply because it is so much less risky and requires less commitment from the record company. Additionally, many dance hits are time-specific, snapshots of a summer spent abroad in foreign superclubs and a memory of good times.

However, be aware that such single deals can really be very small. You might get a flat fee of no more than a couple of thousands pounds. If you manage to create an album of material and then establish a profile for a dance band that supports any further investment, that would all change of course. But the charts are filled with fleeting visits by dance acts, so bear this in mind.

How to become a superstar DJ is a vast and complicated subject, which cannot be covered in depth in this book. I have tried to give you a few starting points and ground rules if you genuinely think this is the career for you. Suffice to say, if you think waiting until you are twenty to become a pop star is unbearable, then you should sell your decks and go stand at the back of the queue. Your name's not down, you're not coming in.

14. FUNDING YOUR CAREER AND LEARNING MORE

'Five years ago, I would get annoyed when my [welfare] cheque arrived a day late. The next thing I know, I'm getting pissed off if my limo didn't turn up.' Seal

THE PRICE OF FAME
Until your million-selling first single hits the number-one slot in a dozen countries, you might be wise to figure out what you are going to live on while your legendary career gets moving.

There are no easy answers to this one, but here are some of the most obvious options:

- starve in a rat-infested cellar and refusing all income other than that generated by your talent as a performer (you stay true to your intentions, maintain your waiflike figure and pale complexion, and avoid all distractions that might get in your way)
- get grants and loans from funding bodies
- find another source of income, such as a job
- sponge off family and friends

Let's look at these one at a time.

STARVING
Well, it doesn't sound great, does it? Nowadays, with the pop world evolved into such a sophisticated, international business, the days of lying in darkened rooms with nothing to eat but a stale crust seem a long way away. But let's face it: most people who pursue a career in pop music fail, or – if they are lucky enough to succeed – they take a long time to earn any real money, so somehow you're going to have to keep yourself alive while you wait for the big bucks to come in. Not for nothing do the music biz veterans say, 'Don't give up the day job.'

Many artists of different persuasions – painters, writers, actors included – decide that to accept any form of income not generated by their craft is actually to compromise their art and dilute its core truths. I am not one of these people. However, many hopefuls think, 'How can

I give myself 100 per cent to my singing career if I'm spending nine hours a day welding bits of metal together?'

If you are earning a little money from your music already and you think you can get loads more work by being available 24/7, then why not go for it? You need to think of some basics. Do I have to pay rent or a mortgage? How much do I spend on food and living expenses per month? Do I need to buy stage gear, guitar strings, costumes? Do I have to pay petrol costs and taxi fares to get to and from gigs? How mad is my dad going to be when I tell him, 'I already have a job, I'm an artiste.'?

Take a month keeping a diary of what you spend your money on. Write it all down, and at the end of the month go through the list – and your bank statement if you have one – and add up what your outgoings are. Then look at your career earnings to date. Which is the higher figure? I bet I know which it is. Can you cut back on costs – not so many nights out or taxis where you could take the bus? Can you get more work than you are actually getting at the moment by hustling and putting your face about town more? Can you live with your family for a year instead of paying rent on an apartment?

If you can make the incoming money match the outgoing money then you are already doing well, and it's great news for your future career that you can not only support yourself now but can handle your money responsibly. Good luck. You'll need it.

GRANTS AND LOANS

This is a minefield, because there are many opportunities for loans, start-up packages and grants from many different sources, and finding them is not always easy. Here are some worthwhile routes to get you started.

The Prince's Trust

The Prince's Trust was started over 25 years ago to help the unemployed, educational underachievers, those in care or ex-offenders, all in many different ways. In 2001, more than thirty thousand people in the UK benefited from their help. If you have a good idea for a business – and your career in music is a business in just the same way as opening a shoe shop is – then the Prince's Trust may be able to offer you a loan of up to £5,000 at very low interest, a grant of up to £3,000, a marketing grant as well as advice, business start-up kits, seminars on running your business and so on. To qualify, you need to be between eighteen and thirty, and you need to make a convincing case that your music career as a business is viable with the help of the trust.

The National Foundation for Youth Music

Usually called 'Youth Music' for short, this is a lottery-funded organisation aiming to make access to music making easier for young people up to and including eighteen years of age in England (it does not, currently, include Northern Ireland, Scotland or Wales). Check out their excellent website for details of their plans to spend £60 million of funding by the end of 2005, at www.youthmusic.org.uk. Much of its activities centre on schools, youth clubs and community centres, but you may well be able to benefit by having a look around their site to see what current projects exist, especially if your own musical activity is currently via a school, club or community centre. It also has frequently updated links to other useful sites, particularly those with regional information.

The bank

Your bank or building society is the obvious place to go if you want to borrow money, but be careful – you can get tied into long-term commitments that are binding, and, just because you are one day going to win a Grammy Award, don't expect your bank manager to agree to a huge overdraft.

Most high street banks and building societies will not let you take out a personal loan until you are eighteen. They will probably expect you to have held an account with them for some time, and will expect to see that that account has been well looked after: no long-term overdrafts left to fester. They will also be likely to want to see that there is regular income streaming into that account, so here's where that job in the burger bar comes in! If you have no income then a bank is unlikely to want to risk its money on a loan to you, but, if you can prove at least some regular longer-term income, then your chances are better.

Never forget that your career in entertainment is a job of work, and running your affairs is merely running your own business. Banks and building societies are excellent places to ask advice on setting up your business, because they recognise that successful businesses build good customers for them. Most branches have a small-business adviser, who can help with advice on all sorts of aspects of setting yourself up in business. They will invariably have a special booklet or package full of relevant information, and it won't do you any harm to make an appointment with the small-business adviser at your local branch and have a chat. You may sense an immediate scepticism with many advisers and, if so, you will probably be wasting your time. However, you will eventually find one who understands that music can be a healthy career and they will be much more likely to talk to you seriously.

Prepare for your meeting. Write a business plan that you can present to the bank. If you were starting a shoe shop, you would explain to them where the shop was going to be, who your clients were likely to be, what the competition in town was, and why your shop would do better than others. You would have researched your costs in setting up and maintaining the business – rents and rates on property, shelving and carpeting, costs of wages, stock and so on – and would forecast how much you would expect to take in revenue from the business, too. A plan like this shows the bank that you have done your homework and understand the business that you are getting yourself into.

It's not as easy to write a business plan for a pop career, obviously, but you could perhaps explain what your targets in the next six months/two years/five years might be (and be realistic!), list how many gigs you have played to date and note down the income from each and the combined income from them all. List your costs – petrol, instruments, hotel rooms, whatever. Work out what you will be able to afford to pay per month in repaying the loan, and again be realistic: there's no point thinking you can repay £300 a month when you are earning £30 a week! Type all this up neatly using a word processor and present it to the business adviser to let him or her know that you are taking your career seriously, that you have managed your affairs well to date, and that you are professional in taking the necessary steps to acquire funding to get you to the next level. Keep a copy for yourself.

It is always wise to open a band bank account, making certain that you need more than one member to sign cheques (especially if the one signatory has a taste for fast cars). That way, you will also be able to approach banks with more credibility and service any loans or funding you receive more precisely. If you are a solo performer, this might still be a good idea so you can manage your funds more carefully.

NESTA
NESTA is the National Endowment for Science, Technology and the Arts. Funded by National Lottery money, it exists to help develop talent,

innovation and creativity in science, technology and the arts. NESTA can help fund projects to turn great new ideas into even better new products. They are not going to buy your stage gear and fund your tour of Scandinavia, but, if you are going to set the music world alight with a new synthesiser that you are developing, if you've invented a new guitar tuner or written an exciting new sampling program, if you've devised an electric flute or wind-up guitar amp, then NESTA may well be able to help you achieve your goals. See their website at www.nesta.org.uk.

Local councils

This is a difficult area for funding because councils operate in many different ways. Most local councils have grants for business development, and you may or may not qualify, depending upon whether you can convince your council that you are a viable 'business' rather than simply an individual seeking a loan for personal development. Check in *Yellow Pages* or online for contact details, and call up the council for advice. As ever, be professional, be smart, be serious and be prepared to get knocked back.

Friends and family

It may seem obvious, but if you need £5,000 to get you off the ground and the bank, the building society and the funding bodies can't help, then approach members of your family. Even if your immediate family of parents, brothers and sisters cannot help, you may well have an uncle, cousin or aunt in a successful business who would be happy to make you a loan on easy terms.

Be professional here too, though – if you do have relatives willing to invest in you, they'll want to know that you are worth their time and money just as much as a bank would, so do all your homework and hit them with a highly polished professional plea, not just a jokey grovel over a plate of chips on Friday night. And tread carefully: money can easily come between previously close family and friends.

GET A JOB

Geri Halliwell was an assistant on a Turkish TV game show; Bryan McFadden from Westlife was a security guard in a burger joint; Jonathan Davis (Korn) was an assistant coroner. Here are some examples of people who still made it to the big time, despite having a day job: Sharlene Spiteri (hairdresser), Elvis Costello (computer programmer), David Bowie (worked in an ad agency), Beck (leaf blower), Nelly Furtado (worked for an alarm company), Madonna (worked in a doughnut store), Britney Spears (worked part-time in her grandma's delicatessen).

All of these jobs supported people who have since become enormously successful, wealthy and famous. Very often a full- or part-time job can be the means by which you are able to continue pursuing your career in music. Put simply, you have to put bread on the table, and, if your singing or playing is not enough to earn a living (which for most unsigned artists it isn't), then you should think about how you will live until that happens. Simple rules will apply. Your job needs to be one that allows you to pursue your career, so if you are playing in clubs five nights a week then a job in a bar working evenings is not going to be much good – get a job that allows working hours to fit your needs.

You could mould the two spheres of your life together and try to get a job that is somehow appropriate to your aspirations in the music biz – if you want to sing in musical theatre, approach the theatres locally and see what jobs they might have available, be they selling ice cream or sweeping the dressing room floors. Working in the theatre will mean that you meet theatre people, theatre managers, agents, other singers and actors. And one day, while singing to yourself when you are sweeping up after the evening performance, the director hears you, and the rest is history . . . (It *does* happen.)

Perhaps try getting work at a local studio, which would have the dual benefit of earning some (small) income and putting you in a position where you can pick up technical knowledge and meet people on the local scene. Working at record companies is also worth thinking about, although competition for even administrative roles within the music industry is fierce. Even a record shop will at least allow you to hear new music all day.

Part-time work may suit you best of all. Pack eggs in boxes, work in a supermarket, fill cars with petrol or work at a car wash, clean office floors . . . There's nothing like a routine job to remind you how great it feels to be up on stage instead! Put an ad in your local paper offering your services for any kind of casual work, or approach local job centres and employment agencies. Check the music and theatre press – such as *Music Week* and the *Stage* (you don't have to subscribe – ask your library to get them for you) for jobs in the industry that will allow you access to people who can help you on your way.

These suggestions may seen rather unglamorous, but it is a simple fact of life that it is going to cost money to get into the music business. One band who have enjoyed enormous success and critical acclaim as possibly the finest British rock act of the last five years are the Scottish group Idlewild. Yet their success all started when they financed their debut single via a student loan.

It was this self-financed single that in turn attracted their manager, Bruce Craigie, to working with the band. 'I was working as a consultant to Deceptive Records/Music,' recalls Bruce, 'and they sent me their student-loan-financed record, "Queen of the Troubled Teens". That showed me a real determination that immediately impressed me. I saw them live and there was an uncertain chaos, but hidden beneath the cacophony were some great melodies.'

In 2002, Idlewild's third album, *The Remote Part*, went into the top five and they headed out on tour supporting Coldplay.

COURSES AND EDUCATION

Can you *learn* to be a pop star? Probably not, but in an industry where you can get taken for a ride more often than a Swedish hitchhiker, the more you have in your toolbox the better you'll do the job. Courses can help you understand the business better, teach you specifics about individual areas in the music biz, and – most importantly – get you more useful contacts.

The courses available are immensely varied and I can only begin to give you an overview here. Many universities and colleges run courses right up to degree level. LIPA, the Liverpool Institute for the Performing Arts, is a good example of a multidisciplined college where you can study lighting, theatre technology, dance, music and lots more in a variety of course situations aimed at performers *and* those who make performances happen. The college also runs – mainly for people in the northwest of England – distance-learning courses lasting for a full year or between two and eight weeks. One course – 'Fine Tune' – is specifically aimed at up-and-coming new bands.

All manner of subjects can be covered, ranging from commercial music (available in Bath, Paisley, Warrington, Westminster and Newcastle, according to the Universities and Colleges Admissions Service for the UK (UCAS) in autumn 2002), contemporary music

(Preston, Leeds and Newcastle) and creative music (Leeds) through to popular music (44 courses listed), popular music performance (Thames Valley) and world music (Leeds), and from colleges and universities from Edinburgh down to Canterbury in Kent. The best place to source information on these courses is the UCAS website (www.ucas.com). Here you can search for the kind of course you want and all the information is given on the college or department that you need to contact. Write to or telephone the institutions you are interested in and ask them for a prospectus, which will then contain all the necessary information that you'll need in order to assess whether or not their course is right for you.

There are also various companies who run shorter, more targeted courses for the music industry in general. Fees vary – from a little over £100 for a one-day course to between £300 and £400 for a three- to six-day course. One such company is Global Entertainment Ltd, based in London. They run courses throughout the year on anything from an overview of the music industry, which puts the industry into a broad perspective covering marketing, branding, songwriting, publishing, sales and distribution, to a course on recording an effective demo. Most of Global's courses are held in London, but they have held them around the UK and intend to broaden their geographical catchment, so they are well worth checking out for more information. Their courses – being short and targeted – are good to take on before you commit yourself to a three-year spell at university. Check in your local area if there are any similar companies you might benefit from working with.

Another excellent resource is The Band Agency, a not-for-profit organisation that offers seminars, masterclasses, band forums and every aspect of advice on a fledgling band's career. They work specifically with unsigned musicians and follow them through to their professional career. Check out more about The Band Agency at www.TheBandAgency.com.

In the London area, you can check out *Floodlight* magazine, which lists all the courses available at government-funded colleges and education centres in all the capital's boroughs. Web surfers and people outside of London can access the same information at *Floodlight's* website at www.floodlight.co.uk, an excellent resource centre that will come up with several pop or rock music courses for you.

Remember, though, that a training course, degree or piece of paper will not give you talent that you already lack. What it will give you is access to people, networks, studios and the sort of information and knowledge that isn't easy to get hold of from your bedroom. You'll meet other musicians by the bucket load, will share ideas and information, will form bands and allegiances that will be useful later on in your career, and, from being a hairbrush-for-microphone karaoke wannabe, you'll become an informed, well-connected, targeted and well-practised hopeful.

If this all sounds a little like staying on too long at school, listen to how the cult drum and bass outfit Fake ended up being played on Radio 1 through being at Durham University. Founder member Jonny Lattimer tells their story.

Prompted by the reaction of people in Durham University, we gave our demo to the agent responsible for dealing with my partner in the band, Tim. She liked our stuff and started promoting it for free. She sent it to Mary-Anne Hobbes at Radio 1, who started playing it a lot and eventually asked us to compile a half-hour mix for her show.

My degrees at Durham have actually been quite irrelevant to my aspirations in music, but the people I've met haven't. From contacts I made I was able to get a job in the music industry to tide me over while I work on my new band.

On a similar note, Belle & Sebastian leaped from a music course on to a 'Best Newcomer' Brit Award in a very short space of time. Their former bass player, Stuart David, traces the origins of their success back to Stow College in Glasgow.

Alan Rankin ran the music course at Stow College and he'd been a popster in the 1980s with the Associates. He whipped up a big buzz about Belle & Sebastian among the contacts he had in the industry. Then it just snowballed. Belle & Sebastian just took off very suddenly. We weren't even aware that we were really a band, yet most of the record companies in Britain wanted to sign us.

Other musicians find that actually playing at universities can boost their career. Be wary, though: this is much harder in recent times. Many such educational establishments have exclusive deals with promotion companies who organise the gigs for them. You might get a chance to open for some of the bigger acts but that is very rare.

Paul Oakenfold is more dubious about the benefits of courses. 'I was self-taught and so are many of my peers,' he says. 'A lot of people frown on too much academic background, so be careful.'

Stuart David left Belle & Sebastian to pursue his own act, Looper, as well as a career as a novelist. Looper have since featured on the soundtrack to the Tom Cruise film, *Vanilla Sky*. Stuart finds the advances of home technology vital to his creativity, something that he honed through education.

When the technology was just coming together to allow you to work with loops of real audio on a PC quite cheaply, I was fascinated. I'd done a year-long course in electronic music at college in 1990, and I'd loved that way of working with loops – but I didn't like the quality of sounds at the time. They were all fake and midi, but, when the technology progressed such that you could work that way with real sounds, that was what I wanted to do.

So don't dismiss further or higher education. It probably won't turn you into Will Young the second you graduate, but it could be just another string to your bow.

Think about it.

15. GENERATING PUBLICITY AND WORKING THE MEDIA

'Journalists from university killed pop music. Now we are bringing it back. We need to be cheered up.' Pete Waterman

Before we go any further, a word of caution. If you are solely interested in being a pure-pop star, then it is highly unlikely that as an unsigned artist you will be able to use the media to strengthen your chances of a record deal. Once you are signed, too, your publicity will be handled by your management, record company and possibly an independent PR company. If you do become a pop star, then you and the media will be close bedfellows throughout your career, at times intimate and on occasions fractious. How you handle and work with the powerful beast that is the modern media can make a colossal difference to you.

However, if you are aiming for a career in a band or a less 'manufactured' genre, then a good working knowledge of the media is an invaluable tool. In the first instance, a clever unsigned artist or band will use the press to generate more interest in them from record companies. Perhaps a classic example of this is the Welsh band Manic Street Preachers, who used a quite brilliant campaign of letter writing to raise their profile. Before the music media had even a chance to hear the Manics' music, they were first bombarded with an amazing selection of venom-filled letters. This was a carefully researched plan. During their early days in South Wales, the band had meticulously kept press files of all the bylined journalists, how they wrote, who they liked, disliked, reviewed and so on.

With this database of names and attitudes, the Manics then started firing off ranting letters to these people, as well as to managers, record-company executives and industry types in general. The handwritten tirades would often stretch to four or five pages, wherein the band would rail against all the evils of the world, and announce their own brilliance. At the start of 1990, the music media were awash with these highly articulate, expertly written manifestos, which were reinforced by quotes from all corners of literature: Marx, Burroughs, Orwell, Greil Marcus . . .

This was bound to attract attention among the music press, who were daily bombarded with dull and formulaic PR-speak. After receiving reams of these letters, journalists would then be phoned up and, their curiosity heightened, invariably spoke to the Manics in person. In this fashion the band were able to attract quite a few media names to that first London gig in Great Portland Street. When journalists did attend a gig, the band would corner them for hours. Philip Hall of Hall Or Nothing PR was one such recipient and his company works with the Manics to this day. Jeff Barrett of Heavenly Records was also given a letter, which he recalled was 'passionate, it was on fire, it wanted to change the world and it really excited me'. He later signed them to a two single record deal.

This campaign is truly one of the great music-business PR stunts and I am not suggesting that you should be capable of such a unique and innovative masterplan. However, you should not be ignorant of a medium that will at times be almost as pivotal to your success as your music.

Nick White runs his own PR and press agency, Smash Press, which looks after many up-and-coming artists including Princess Superstar. He feels that many aspiring stars should arm themselves with a basic knowledge of the media.

> There seems to be a lack of awareness of where the artist fits in. Usually this manifests itself as 'everything in the chart is shit and we're better than all that'. Very rarely do I come across unsigned talent that sees how they will fit in with the general music scene. They are so into their own music, their sense of what's going on around them is pretty much restricted to their own vision of themselves. Don't be overconfident of your own ability. You need to be willing to look beyond your own image to see what makes other groups press friendly.

Even for pure pop, it never hurts to have an awareness of what other music is out there, even if you are not influenced in any way by that. Don't forget, if you hate a performer so intensely that they make you sing another style or write in a different way, you've been influenced! How do you get this knowledge? By getting out there and playing live, by networking and by reading the press.

If you are a band that will be aiming to win over the ranks of the music media, you need to get a knowledge and awareness *immediately*. How do they review bands? Who likes what style of music? Which known acts have they championed? Nick White thinks this is vital.

New bands have to be very aware of continuously changing press tastes – what works now won't necessarily work in three months' time. They have to study the press and see what's being written about and why. Does the band getting the most coverage look like fashion models? Do they have a top-forty hit? Have they been getting amazing coverage without any releases? Have they been getting incredible live reviews? Which papers are writing the most enthusiastic articles? Really good-looking press photos help but there has to be some sort of 'angle' for the press to be interested in at an early stage. Princess Superstar was very aware of the media. She'd released three albums, nurtured a credible image for herself and connected with very influential journalists at *NME* before the hit single 'Bad Babysitter' was a smash.

Julian Carrera from Hall Or Nothing works with bands such as Stereophonics, Feeder and Super Furry Animals. He has this advice:

The local media are your best bet at an early stage. You need to be quite brave, stick your neck on the block, send your stuff into local papers. The best way to do that is to phone them up and badger them. These local writers do like to see bands from their area do well. If you think your town hasn't ever had a really good music scene, then that can help, because the writers will be keen to start something off. You should be able to sew up the local press on your own and, if you're not doing that, then you might want to question your drive and ambition. Maybe delegate someone in the band to just do the press, but don't ignore it.

So is it worth paying for PR a little later on in an unsigned act's career? 'Could be, yes,' says Nick. 'You might be able to strike a deal with a PR company to do your press for nothing until you get signed, at which point they would then take a percentage or go on a regular retainer.' Bear in mind, though, that this is unusual – but, if the PR company in question is completely bowled over by your demo, who knows?

Damian Harris of Skint Records urges you to remember that journalists receive a lot of approaches, so your own music has to make a good impression and stand out if you're to get them involved. He adds,

Consider also that the dance scene is all about word of mouth and that can be better than any press campaign. We didn't use a press company for ages. So work your club, get people talking about it. Don't go too soon, though. We had a core catalogue of ten records before people started to hear about us nationally, so we were ready for the leap. Once you've got the word of mouth going crazy, all sorts of opportunities will start to open up. You are aiming for that moment when someone gets your record and says, 'Blimey, have you heard about this?'

Nik Moore does publicity for bands such as Motörhead and has worked with Badly Drawn Boy, too, and he is adamant that professional media help can be vital.

Initially, it's fine for a band to contact publications to get exposure, but once they are serious it is quite essential to get someone on board as a publicist. My thinking is this: these days record deals are *very* few and far between. However, there are still the same amount of bands battling for space on the radio and in magazines, so if you hire a publicist you are working with someone who actually knows the important people and can get honest feedback for you.

'The problem is, Nik,' I hear you say, 'I get three pounds fifty an hour stacking shelves and I've heard a good press officer can cost around fifteen hundred quid a month.' Nik replies,

Fair point. Two answers to that. Firstly, you might find a publicist who works for nothing on the strength that they believe in you so much that they'll work on your behalf. Then, when you do get a deal they'll be hired and enjoy the financial benefit thereafter. Unfortunately, as record companies are increasingly taking press in-house, this is a rare offer nowadays, but it can still happen.

Secondly, I speak to tons of bands who say, 'We have only got five hundred pounds and that's got to pay for the advert in *NME*.' I always say, 'Well, no one reads the adverts in the *NME*: they read the articles. If no one's ever heard of you, a quarter-page advert saying you are touring is pointless. Whereas, if you pay me five hundred pounds, at least you have someone working on your behalf to try to get you free coverage, single reviews in music papers and interviews and features, which is far more credible. A good PR can really help lead the horse to water.

WATCHING PAINT DRY

As an aspiring pop star, you must think about the process of your music being covered in the media, both before and after you are signed. Being an entertaining interviewee and having a great personality can make or break your career, even if you are obviously talented. Journalists will be drawn to you; they will want to spend time with you. After all, they have a job of work to do and, if they can make it more interesting, they will. By contrast, if a conversation with you is the definition of tedium itself, look at it from their point of view – they will be in and out of the interview as quickly as you can say 'mind-numbing'.

Natalie Appleton's experience in All Saints and Appleton is that promotion is 90 per cent of the job.

Kids see the singing and the dancing, the fun parts, but they don't see the travelling, the promotion, interviews, the huge amount of flying. I'm scared to fly but I have to, around the world, all the time. The fun part is 10 per cent, the rest is promotion and there's only so much you can talk about the music, the band, what your plans are. You find yourself thinking, 'What the hell am I doing this for? Just so I can talk about it?' Sometimes you might only get one day in the month of actual performing.

WORKING RADIO

Radio can be even more difficult for unsigned artists. I have split this section into the three key levels, but at this stage it is mostly to give you an awareness of how the radio industry works. You need to know.

STUDENT RADIO

These stations provide a good opportunity to get radio experience in the form of sessions or interviews and perhaps some airtime if your demo is good enough. They are generally always short-staffed and desperate for content and new material. Plus, the DJs and programmers are music fanatics – that's why they're involved. At the same time, you need to consider the market you are preaching to. If you are courting a late-night hard-rock DJ at a campus station, are his or her listeners likely appreciate your desire to be the next H from Steps?

Craig Pilling is a DJ on the nationally broadcast Student Broadcast Network Radio and offers a telling insight into the difficulties of working student, local or even national radio to your benefit.

Some student stations are better than others but most are dedicated and professional-sounding outfits. Don't think your material can be of lower quality because it's student radio, because that won't work. I've come across many unsigned acts through student radio. It won't be a given that you will get on, but having said that, people do just turn up at the radio station, give us a cassette and if we like them we'll get them in for a chat, cram all their equipment into our little studio – and corridors! – and take it away!

Student radio also gives you a good media apprenticeship in interviewing, working with music insiders, fitting in around programme schedules and so on, says Craig.

Not everyone is good at talking to the media. If you are a solo performer, you need to learn quick. If you are a band, find out who is the mouthpiece, who is good at gobbing off, and let them do the interviews. Chances are it is the front person. If you become successful you will need to know about all these skills.

LOCAL RADIO
Most local radio stations are now run by much larger corporations, so programming rules are almost as restrictive as for national stations. So you may find it very difficult to get exposure there. That said, many local radio stations have late-night shows that do showcase regional talent and some even sponsor or promote talent shows.

Target your DJ or radio-show producer carefully. Get names first, but appreciate that it is a long shot. Craig Pilling reinforces this view.

Unless you are great friends with the head of music who does all the bookings for the bands and decides what gets played on the radio, there is very little space for unsigned acts. There are a few opportunities, though – BBC Radio Lancashire used to do a show that was on weekend evenings and featured local bands, so look out for something similar in your area.

If you spot a possible opening, phone the head of music and say, 'I'm in a band and appreciate that you have a play list to follow, but do you have any shows that are open to cassettes to be sent in?' Sometimes it might even be like a demo slot, just one song. It has got to be worth a try.

NATIONAL RADIO

In reality, this is a virtual nonstarter. Send your tape in at you peril. These stations are very strictly controlled and programming lists are almost sacrosanct. However, individual DJs may accept tapes and perhaps pass you on to contacts they know. But do be realistic. If you mail your demo to Dr Fox, he probably won't call up Simon Cowell that afternoon.

People called radio pluggers are paid large sums of money by all the major labels to promote their clients' records to national and regional stations. That is what you are up against. Despite this, there are a few select shows fronted by people like John Peel on BBC Radio 1 that always appreciate music being sent in. People like Peel can play whatever they want. If it's good enough, he'll play it. That's the nature of the show.

Don't be disheartened by all this. Radio is something that will, mainly, come into play only when you have your record deal. By then, of course, it will be vital to your career. Until that happens, though, getting a useful knowledge of radio can only be of help.

And before you ask, yes, the Chocolate Speedway Riders *did* manage to get on radio. Problem was, there was an unfortunate misunderstanding between us and the producer of the show over the use of the word 'classic' in our bio. We ended up being cut off air on a West Midlands country-and-western station halfway through a searing rendition of our live favourite, 'How Can You Lie There and Think of England When You Don't Even Know Who's In the Team?'

16. MISCELLANEOUS

'I don't know anything about music. In my line of work you don't have to.' Elvis Presley

MUSIC HISTORY AND YOUR INFLUENCES

There is an old adage that says 'talent borrows but genius steals'. Before you think I'm about to give you a boring history lesson, let me explain how those old records and performers you think only your dad likes can help you become a pop star.

Since the advent of rock 'n' roll in the 1950s, music has been an endless pattern of innovation coupled with recycling. For every spark of genius like the Beatles there were a thousand derivative or copycat bands. What every major star has in common is, almost without exception, a knowledge of what has gone before. If you ignore the past, you may well have no future.

Don't tell me that history is boring. Rock 'n' roll is the most incendiary of all art forms. I am hardly asking you to go and draw pie charts. That said, you do not need to be a music boffin to become a star. It just helps to have a little extra up your sleeve. You can start by checking out any artists your current favourite bands cite as their own influences. Buy the CDs, perhaps read a book or magazine article on them. In turn, other names will crop up and, if you feel suitably inclined, you can trace those, too. You can involve yourself as much or as little with this as you please. What you are doing is arming yourself with a much broader knowledge and sphere of influence. If you think pop music began when the Spice Girls first hit number one, you may well still become a star, but you are missing out on so much that could really help you.

Louis Walsh feels that many of the hopefuls he sees are just too narrow-minded in terms of musical knowledge. 'Broaden that knowledge,' he suggests. 'If you want to hear great singers, don't just listen to Radio 1. Listen to Frank Sinatra, Tony Bennett, Elvis, Dusty Springfield – these are great, great singers. Check out the Burt Bacharach catalogue, early Beatles, Roy Orbison – just widen your horizons.'

The top songwriter Oskar Paul suggests another oft-maligned genre. 'It doesn't hurt to listen to classical,' he says. 'It has all the same principles, more or less. Mozart, for example, was a great pop writer! His melodies are very catchy and singable. You can remember the tunes very easily. So he was definitely a pop writer at the time.'

Once you have enriched your sphere of music, don't be afraid to slice off the best bits that inspire you. 'Being derivative and influenced is not a sin,' says Tony Wadsworth of EMI.

I think at the beginning of Radiohead's career it was pretty clear they had been listening to a lot of U2. In turn, Coldplay would be the first to admit they are massive fans of Radiohead. Idlewild are very special but it is obvious that they listen to REM. Being influenced isn't the issue in itself. It doesn't mean you can't be unique. I think it is what you bring in addition to that. For example, Radiohead very quickly developed their own style on their second album such that, by the third record, *OK Computer*, they were sounding unique. Make sure you bring something fresh to your performance and sound.

Any credible artist is usually a pretty huge music fan. For example, Damon Albarn has got an incredible knowledge of music and always did have, even before he was signed. It is not just a recent dalliance: from the beginning he was influenced by music that was pretty obscure. Some of these people are huge record collectors.

With Robbie Williams, too, his influences are very broad, coming from areas you don't normally associate with a pop star, namely Frank Sinatra, Dean Martin, Sammy Davis Jr. So you can learn from that, listen to artists outside of your favourite genres, soak up a broader palette of sounds and styles. You don't have to be influenced but the knowledge and variety can only help.

Surprisingly, perhaps, Geri Halliwell also impressed Tony Wadsworth with her musical knowledge.

When I first met her she was very driven, very focused, but memorably really passionate about her influences, like pop and movie stars from her teenage years were key, such as Blondie. Yet she was coming at these influence as a fan and that gave her a real energy. She mixed those influences with a clear perception of her own bigger picture. Even early on, those influences helped her strategise all the time, so it was never just a song: there would also be an idea for a video, plus how it might be performed live and so on. Don't underestimate the value of good influences.

Image and presentation are just as likely to be influenced by the past as your music is. It may be an artist whom you're not at all interested in musically, but go and look at their image and see if you can learn and take ideas from them. The top photographer Jill Furmanovsky thinks a knowledge of what has gone before is key to a new act's or artist's look and cites Bob Dylan as a good example. 'He has had to invent lots of looks to get noticed,' she says. 'People might think, looking at him, that he has no image at all. Yet he has probably the most carefully constructed image of all time.'

Liam Gallagher openly cites Ian Brown of the Stone Roses as an inspiration and the similarities between the two in performance are striking, but Liam managed to add that something extra of his own. As Jill says, 'Plagiarism, if that is the right word, is absolutely essential in terms of presentation.' Whatever age or genre you are in, look outside of that generation, that type of music, take pieces of more diverse areas and bring them into your presentation.

However, there is a contrasting note of caution to this argument, best expressed by the top designer and music expert Malcolm Garrett.

I think a little knowledge can be a bad thing. An innocent lack of understanding of history will give you more courage to follow your convictions. At a young age the music is life-forming, the embodiment of a person, and at that age you can't possibly have a broad knowledge of music history. History can be a burden, it can stop you doing things. You will think, 'I can't do that – it's already been done.' If you are not encumbered by history then you might be better off. That arrogance of youth will fire you up with a huge energy from which something will emerge. You may cover ground which has been covered before, but invariably if you are talented your new music will be right for your time.

The same applies with fashion history, really. That, too, can be a burden. Besides, you all have a bit of history – you've heard something that you like or that you aspire to. But this obsession with doing something different can be just too suffocating. Just add something of your own innate creativity, splice in your flavour. When you hear a fantastic record from years ago, don't think, 'Damn, they've already done that', because your energy will be killed. Instead be inspired to take it one step further and find your own voice.

MERCHANDISE

Whether you are a solo performer or a band/group, in the early stages of your career, you need to be meticulously careful with your finances (see also Chapters 4 and 11). Even if you sign a record deal, it could be a very long time – often years – before any decent money starts to trickle through. Therefore, you need a two-pronged approach to financing your dream:

● Cut costs wherever and whenever possible on elements that do not compromise the quality of your music or talent.
● Source alternative means of income.

We've already covered starving, day jobs, grants and loans, but one final avenue is merchandise or, more specifically at this point, T-shirts. You may well think, 'But I'm a super diva. What has this got to do with my art, my genius?' When you are struggling to find money to pay for the train to get to a gig, it will have everything to do with it, so put your feet back on the ground and listen.

You should never undervalue the benefit of selling merchandise. Acts that play huge venues to a capacity of tens of thousands might pick up an extra £250,000 from merchandise sales. They don't ignore its potential, so why should you? First, T-shirts can generate revenue. Gary Pettet is a director of MFL and has years of high-profile merchandising behind him for acts such as Travis, Stereophonics, Coldplay, the Doves and numerous cult US bands such as Reel Big Fish and Rival Schools.

When an act starts touring [says Gary], the sale of a few T-shirts and perhaps some CDs can provide a vital source of extra income, quite often more than they get from the actual shows themselves. With this in mind, you have to consider very carefully the cost of producing those shirts. There is no point making some vast artistic statement if it means you have to sell thousands of extra shirts to break even. That extra money might keep you on the road for a few more shows and maybe at the very last one of those there might be someone in the audience who could give you your big break. So don't dismiss it.

T-shirts are printed on a silk screen with a fine gauge. This means that you will have to have a 'screen' for each colour and a film. A T-shirt printer might quote you a price for one shirt, but you also need to allow for setup costs. Once you have set a shirt up and done one run, these setup costs will not be repeated. You don't have to be Richard Branson, therefore, to realise that it is best to find a good-selling shirt quickly, and stick to it. That first run might only be 25 or 50 shirts – bear in mind that, if your last gig was to four old-age pensioners, the lower unit costs for printing 300 shirts might be somewhat irrelevant. Remember, this is your business.

'Many artists starting out make the big mistake of paying for a graphic artist or similar to design a shirt for them,' says Gary. He adds,

> More often than not, the costs are prohibitive and there is the additional danger that what works on an album sleeve looks totally wrong on a shirt. Think the design through yourself and, above all, keep it simple. I see so many bands get carried away with multicolours, special colours, metallic prints, all sorts of stuff. Half the time it is lost on the buyer, anyway, and all it achieves is a lot of difficulty controlling quality and little or no profit. Simple logos like Oasis and Motörhead can be hugely popular and not stupidly expensive to produce.

As you become more successful, you need to be aware that factors other than production costs will creep into your sums. Venues for larger acts typically ask for up to 25 per cent of the gross income from shirts, plus VAT. This is a bone of contention with many artists, especially if they feel the venue is making very little effort to sell the shirts. So keep an eye out, monitor how things are being displayed, be proactive.

Another point to consider is that T-shirts are a walking advert; they are part of your branding. In 1990, the underground music scene was filled with loud, brilliantly conceived shirts for a band called Ned's Atomic Dustbin. The shirts usually centred on a distinctive wheel-of-fire logo and were complemented by large, block slogans. Everyone seemed to have one. The amount of advance publicity and buzz this generated around Ned's was enormous. Of course it also created revenue and helped fund their early exhaustive touring schedules. Ned's may not be your type of music, but you would do well to learn from their merchandising strategy. It worked.

YOU AND THE INTERNET

By now you understand that a successful recording artist will use whatever tools are at their disposal to make their career happen. The Internet is one such tool. Again, if you want to be in the new Westlife, having your own site may be of limited use, but, as a relatively cheap and easy means of spreading the word about your act, it should not be ignored.

Your website is up to you, there is no formula. Obviously, there should be certain elements: info on the where and when of shows, perhaps some audio samples if you have the technology, links to other similar artists, perhaps. There is a lot of controversy about how downloading songs cripples music and, for record companies and artists who already make a living from their music, this is a very real and serious issue. However, for you as an unsigned artist, giving bits of your music away at this stage can only help. It is a great chance to spread the gospel.

Stephen Barnes of Upshot Promotions has a word of caution about some of the promotional ideas hopefuls use the Web for.

Certainly get your band or own domain name. Also, use the Web as a research tool for agents, record companies, pressing plants, message boards for contacts and references and so on. Email, too, makes your life easier for contacting record-business players. It is not too intrusive, people can reply briefly and it keeps that channel open. The MP3 sites that are out there are helpful to a degree, but I am cynical. I think a lot of those acts are low quality. They tend to be bedroom boffins, too, although I know some acts have been helped in some way. There is certainly no harm putting your music up there, though.

Malcolm Garrett has designed websites for such acts as Oasis, and his advice is to keep it simple.

At the root of the site should be something interesting. It should embody the personality of yourself or the band. You could also use it to extend your fan base outside of your immediate geographic locale, for example by sending live samples to someone in Edinburgh if you only ever play in Portsmouth. Remember that, when young music fans discover a new singer or act, they feel very protective.

I call this whole aspect your 'the secret society'. Buzzcocks termed it slightly differently as 'the Secret Public', which was the name of their fan club, and that really typifies that aspect of new music. The website can therefore generate a buzz and a forum about a performer or band far and wide that otherwise might not be possible. The site should be your secret society's vehicle.

[Iron] Maiden might not be your music but their website is phenomenal. When I did their website, which admittedly was massively comprehensive, we almost had meltdown when it went live because there were so many hits. We nearly brought the whole Web down! Of course, they already have a huge success, but you can learn from stories like that to generate success in the early stages.

Malcolm suggests that if you are confident enough to try out various Internet avenues, you can only benefit.

Virtual bands (Gorillaz), websites, webcasts of live shows, mail-outs – these are all things that can be used to your advantage. Instead of looking at the Web as a medium that is suffocating music, look at it as opening loads of new opportunities for you. That is very exciting and you should make the most of that. The modern star is much more of a multimedia artist, so it can't hurt that you are aware of that. Even if you have no deal, this is something to educate yourself about for the future.

ROCK 'N' ROLL

Before you head off into your future career as a pop superstar, one final word of caution. Whether you are a club singer or a global megastar, you will encounter varying amounts of excess and temptation – rock 'n' roll. If I started giving you a list of all the examples of excess and debauchery that the music biz can boast, this book would be the largest publication ever printed and you would be decades past your sell-by date before you finished reading it. Some of it would be hilarious, some of it fascinating, much of it dreadful.

This is not the book to go into that detail but, suffice to say, would you take copious amounts of drugs if you were going for an interview for a job at a bank? Would you turn up to a big presentation to a client completely drunk? Of course not. This is your business.

Peer pressure will play a part and it is your call, not mine, on what you decide to do. Just be aware that it can have serious consequences for both you and your career. My best piece of advice is to read a biography of any of the big bands. There you will find a whole range of views and experiences from which you can learn and make up your own mind.

Louis Walsh offers some sage advice for you to think about before you finally go out there on your own.

The music business has pitfalls. I am anti-drugs and -drink. Avoid both if you are trying to succeed. Drink socially by all means, but you have to look after yourself physically as well as mentally. You wouldn't realise but Bono, Springsteen, Mick Jagger and scores of stars like that look after themselves. It goes with the territory that if you have longevity you look after yourself mentally and physically. Geri looks after herself fantastically well, mind and body. So does Kylie. You are like an athlete, so you have to prepare yourself.

AFTERWORD

So now you know.

Do you still want to become a pop star? Don't tell me: I know the answer.

If you do make it as a pop star, you will have somehow secured a creative, demanding, bizarre and rewarding job that is enjoyed by a very select few. If you don't make it as a pop star, I guarantee that along the way you will meet some amazing people, a fair share of odd ones and the occasional shark. You may end up in a job you never even knew existed, like writing books about pop music.

Whether you make it or not, and I *sincerely* hope you do, have a fantastic time.

It's up to you now.

'You have to have belief, belief, belief'

APPENDIX A: USEFUL ORGANISATIONS

This book is not intended to be a comprehensive directorybut here are a few useful organisations that may be able to help you out.

Musicians' Union
National Office
60–62 Clapham Road
London SW9 0JJ
Tel: 020 7582 5566
Fax: 020 7582 9805
www.musiciansunion.org.uk

Agents' Association
54 Keyes House
Dolphin Square
London SW1V 3NA
Tel: 020 7834 0515
Fax: 020 7821 0261
www.agents-uk.com

Association of Music Industry
   Accountants
Unity House
205 Euston Road
London NW1 2AY
Tel: 020 7383 9200
Fax: 020 7383 9201

International Association of
   Entertainment Lawyers
45–51 Whitfield Street,
London W1P 5RU
Tel: 020 7631 1050
Fax: 020 7436 2744
www.iael.org

Music Managers' Forum
1 Glenthorne Mews
115A Glenthorne Road
London W6 0LJ
Tel: 020 7741 2555
Fax: 020 7741 4856

Music Publishers' Association
3rd Floor, Strandgate
18–20 York Buildings
London WC2N 6JU

International Songwriters'
Association
37b New Cavendish Street
London W1N
Tel: 020 7486 5353
Fax: 020 7486 2094

Generator North East
Black Swan Court
69 Westgate Road
Newcastle NE1 1SG
Tel: 0191 245 0099
Fax: 0191 245 0144

Based in the northeast of England (though its advice is good for you wherever you may live), sponsored by the Arts Council, Musicians' Union and other key funding bodies, Generator (www.generator.org.uk) is an organisation and fun website offering sound and entertainingly written advice on becoming a pop star or developing your band.

Stagecoach
www.stagecoach.co.uk
Tel: 0870 241 5676

The Band Agency
22 Paradise Street,
Cambridge CB1 1DR
Tel: 01223 514932
www.TheBandAgency.com

Xplosive is the studio where Blazin' Squad recorded their demo. Contact them via: www.xplosiverecords.co.uk

The Stage Newspaper Limited
47 Bermondsey Street
London SE1 3XT
Tel: 020 7403 1818
Fax: 020 7357 9287
www.thestage.co.uk

www.helpforbands.com is a unique interactive site offering all kinds of advice, direction and support – often a case of sharing information with others – for unsigned bands. Visit the website for further information.

OTHER WEBSITES

www.natlotcomm.gov.uk – National Lottery Commission
www.artscouncil.org.uk – Arts Council of England
www.ccc-acw.org.uk – Arts Council of Wales
www.sac.org.uk – Scottish Arts Council
www.nesta.org.uk – National Endowment for Science, Technology and the Arts

APPENDIX B: MANAGEMENT CONTRACTS

This will set out the basis on which the relationship between the artist and the manager will be conducted, what services the manager will provide and how he will be paid for his work.

Such contracts are often thought (mainly by managers) to provide very weak protection for managers, because, if there is a fall-out, the manager cannot force the artist to honour the terms of the contract if he doesn't want to. In this respect it is similar to an employment contract in that, if an employee leaves his job without giving the required amount of notice, the employer cannot force him to work the notice period. The only remedy the employer (or in this case manager) would have would be to sue the employee (or in this case artist) for damages. If the action is successful, the employee/artist would then have to pay the employer/manager a sum equal to the financial loss the employer/manager has suffered. In a situation where a successful artist breaches his or her management contract, this sum could be substantial. However, the manager would still be in a position where he was effectively left out in the cold.

Because of this, managers sometimes try to protect their position by entering agreements whereby the manager takes ownership of the copyright in the artist's songs and recordings and then 'licenses' them to record and/or publishing companies. This gives much stronger protection to the manager, but artists should avoid these types of contract at all costs unless there are exceptional circumstances, and should never sign up without first consulting a music lawyer.

TERMS OF A MANAGEMENT CONTRACT

Management contracts are fairly straightforward affairs for the personal services of the manager. However, there are a number of key important provisions that an artist should be aware of. The ability to negotiate the most favourable terms for the artist will depend on the relative bargaining power of the artist and the manager.

The following terms merit particular attention:

THE TERM

Commonly, management contracts run for between three and five years. This is referred to as the 'term'. However, they often contain a provision whereby the artist can get out of the contract if the manager has not secured a record and/or publishing deal within a given period (usually twelve months). This is the manager's primary function at the early stage of an artist's career and in the event that he is not able to perform that function then the artist should be free to go and find a manager who can.

TERRITORY

It is important to establish the geographical scope of a management agreement. Often the appointment will cover the artist's activities throughout the world. However, a manager may well be familiar with the way in which the industry operates in Britain and even Europe, but have no experience in the United States, where the music business is conducted in a very different way. Accordingly, it is common, especially with successful artists, for managers to be appointed for territories in which they have good contacts and particular experience of the industry. However, with new artists a manager is almost always appointed on a worldwide basis.

SCOPE

All management agreements should have a clause that sets out which elements of the artist's career the manager is appointed to manage (and therefore get paid for). At its broadest, the clause will express that a manager is appointed in respect of all the artist's activities within the entertainment industry, which will include not just recording and songwriting activities but television appearances, acting, producing, remixing, merchandising and so forth.

At its narrowest, it may be that the manager is appointed to manage an artist only in respect of recording and songwriting. This will depend in part on the bargaining position between the parties and on the manager's experience in specific areas. For example, a manager may well be experienced in negotiating recording and publishing agreements but know little or nothing about sponsorship or negotiating merchandising licences.

COMMISSION

This is how the manager gets paid. The manager will earn commission on all of the income derived from product over which he is appointed. During the term of the contract this is almost always 20 per cent of everything the artist earns after the payment of expenses such as recording costs, advertising costs, equipment costs and touring costs (although touring income is sometimes commissioned at a higher rate).

Once the contract has come to an end, the manager will usually continue to receive commission on any money the artist makes as a result of work done during the term of the contract. However, this will usually be at a reducing rate. So, for example, if an artist released an album during the term, the manager would receive 20 per cent of the income from that album. However, after the contract has ended, the manager would receive a reduced commission on sales of the first album. This post-term commission usually reduces gradually from 20 per cent to nothing over a ten- to fifteen-year period. This provision in the agreement is generally referred to as the 'sunset clause'. In some cases the manager will receive a low level of commission in perpetuity.

EXPENSES

The artist will invariably have to agree to pay the manager's expenses incurred in promoting the artist's career. In order to protect the artist, these can often be capped so that the manager can spend only a fixed amount each month (initially about £500). If he wants to spend a larger amount – for example, on setting up a tour – he should obtain the artist's approval. These expenses will usually be paid only out of money actually earned by the artist and will not usually be recoverable as a debt if the artist doesn't make any money. In that case, the manager loses his investment and this is essentially why management agreements are regarded by managers as high-risk.

ACCOUNTING

Hopefully, during the life of the management agreement, the artist will make considerable sums of money. That is, after all, the reason for entering the management agreement in the first place. That money must be properly handled and an accountant will usually be appointed to manage an artist's finances. The issue is whether the artist controls and collects the income and pays the manager's commission or whether the manager controls and collects all of the money, retains his commission and pays the balance to the artist. Obviously this is of particular importance when a dispute arises between the manager and the artist.

Broadly speaking, the person with control of the money is in a stronger position than the person who is owed the money. Therefore, it is usually preferable from an artist's point of view to negotiate a position where the artist collects the money and pays the manager.

RESTRICTIONS ON THE MANAGER

The management agreement should stipulate that the manager cannot enter contracts on behalf of the artist without the artist's consent (except for minor contracts: for example, for one-off live performances or television appearances). This effectively prevents the manager from entering recording or publishing agreements on behalf of the artist unless the artist has first approved the terms of those agreements. Similarly, the manager should not be able to subcontract his obligations without the artist's consent. This provision is particularly relevant where sub-managers are appointed for foreign territories, for example the United States.

KEY-MAN CLAUSE
Where the manager is employed by a large management company and the management contract is between the artist and the company, then a clause should be inserted so that, if the manager leaves the company, then the artist is entitled to end the agreement. This ensures that the artist does not end up being managed by a stranger.

MANAGER'S DUTIES
The management agreement should always contain a clause that a manager will use his best efforts to further the career of the artist and provide the services normally provided by a first-class manager in the music industry.

TERMINATION
It is important that the artist does not end up being managed by a liquidator or receiver, who will generally have no experience of the music industry or artist management. To prevent this, a provision should be included in the agreement such that the artist is entitled to terminate the agreement in the event that the manager is made bankrupt or a receiver is appointed over his affairs. In that event the artist will be free to terminate the agreement and find another manager.

MISCELLANEOUS
A useful source for artists searching for management is the Music Managers' Forum, a trade body that represents music managers and will introduce artists looking for representation to potentially interested managers. The Music Managers' Forum currently has a membership in excess of five hundred managers and can be contacted through its website at www.ukmmf.net.

© Nigel Gilroy, Davenport Lyons, 2002

INDEX